how to be

blessed and
highly favored

ADDITIONAL BOOKS BY
MICHELLE McKINNEY HAMMOND

What to Do Until Love Finds You

Secrets of an Irresistible Woman

The Power of Femininity

His Love Always Finds Me

If Men Are Like Buses, Then How Do I Catch One?

Get a Love Life

What Becomes of the Brokenhearted?

Prayer Guide for the Brokenhearted

Intimate Thoughts, Whispered Prayers

how to be

blessed and
highly favored

Michelle McKinney Hammond

WATERBROOK
PRESS

HOW TO BE BLESSED AND HIGHLY FAVORED
PUBLISHED BY WATERBROOK PRESS
2375 Telstar Drive, Suite 160
Colorado Springs, Colorado 80920
A division of Random House, Inc.

All Scripture quotations, unless otherwise indicated, are taken from the *Holy Bible, New International Version®*. NIV®. Copyright © 1973, 1978, 1984 by International Bible Society. Used by permission of Zondervan Publishing House. All rights reserved. Scripture quotations marked (ASV) are taken from the *American Standard Version*. Scripture quotations marked (KJV) are taken from the *King James Version*. Scripture quotations marked (NASB) are taken from the *New American Standard Bible®*. © Copyright The Lockman Foundation, 1960, 1962, 1963, 1968, 1971, 1972, 1973, 1975, 1977. Used by permission. (www.Lockman.org).

Italics in Scripture quotations reflect the author's added emphasis.

ISBN 1-57856-449-2

Published in association with the literary agency of Alive Communications, Inc., 7680 Goddard Street, Suite 200, Colorado Springs, Colorado 80920.

Library of Congress Cataloging-in-Publication Data
McKinney Hammond, Michelle, 1957–
    Blessed and highly favored : living richly under the smile of God / by Michelle
    McKinney Hammond.— 1st ed.
        p. cm.
    ISBN 1-57856-449-2
        1. Christian life.   I. Title.
    BV4501.3 .M37 2001
    248.4—dc21   2001026276

Printed in the United States of America
2001—First Edition

10 9 8 7 6 5 4 3 2

My heart, my soul, my everything
belongs to the One who has given His all for me.
Lord, my most urgent prayer is that I will be responsible
for more smiles on Your face than tears from Your heart.
May I bless You in all I say and do.

To my parents and siblings
who are my greatest blessing and delight.
You bless my life with the most important ingredient:
endless love.

contents

acknowledgments

To my new family at WaterBrook: I'm excited about our future together. Thank you for acknowledging my heart and insisting on passion.

Erin Healy: You, my precious editor, are an angel! Thank you for the questions, observations, and encouragement. Truly two are better than one. I thank God for you.

Laura Wright, my production editor, thank you for making me tell "it" like it is.

Chip McGregor, thank you for your constant sensitivity and care. And for arranging a beautiful marriage.

To the faithful twelve: You know who you are. Thank you for praying, pushing, prodding, provoking, listening, correcting…well… You know all that you do. You are loved and appreciated.

it's a wonderful life

EMBRACING THE CONCEPT
OF EXTRA-DIMENSIONAL BLESSINGS

"Fear not, little flock; for it is your Father's good
pleasure to *give* you the *kingdom.*"

LUKE 12:32 (KJV)

The young man peered over the containers he was stacking to answer my
question. "Sure, we carry that yogurt. As a matter of fact, I'm switching the
merchandise on that brand right now. Here, take these. They're still good.
Just tell them at the checkout that I said you could have them for free."

"Wow! Thanks," I said. Gleefully I headed toward the front of the store,
my arms loaded with several pint-size containers. As I conveyed the message to the sales clerk, my girlfriend (who was ahead of me in line *paying*
for her yogurt) said, "How do you always manage to do that? Girl, you
must have an invisible sign on you somewhere that says, 'Give me
everything for free!' "

I have a confession to make. I am spoiled. Terribly, terribly spoiled. It's
true. I have been the recipient of such freebies as yogurt, free rent, a beautiful baby grand piano, and well, you name it! And that's just the tangible,

in-your-hands end of the spectrum. I could go on and on about God's loving guidance, His special way of letting me know I have His undivided attention (at least it feels that way), or the favor He gives me with others. I choose to name all these things gifts from God. Some of my blessings have been material, and others have been incredible opportunities that some would view as serendipitous moments, but I see my Father's hand in the midst of it all.

Looking back over my life, I can honestly say that God has pretty much given me everything I've ever asked Him for, from the easy to the seemingly impossible. My list of unfulfilled requests is a short one comprised of things I still anticipate receiving in His perfect time. Why am I so confident? It certainly isn't because I'm more spiritual than the next person. I know many people who pray more, read their Bible more, and simply know more about God than I do. On the contrary: As I have sought to understand why some folks are blessed more abundantly than others, God's Word has confirmed for me that His ultimate desire is for *all* of us to live a blessed life—one that overflows with His rich provision and goodness as we cooperate with His Spirit to become more and more like Christ. I also discovered that being a super-Christian is not a prerequisite to being super-blessed. There—now you can breathe a sigh of relief along with me! However, God's Word does give us some keys to accessing the deep riches of God's blessing, and I plan to share with you in the coming pages what I've learned.

"Blessed and highly favored!" That's the enthusiastic response I often receive when I ask people, "How are you?" It has become one of the favorite sayings of the day, a mantra of sorts as we seek to have a positive confession. This particular response, however, always gives me cause to pause and reflect. *Do these people really know what they're saying? Do they know what is required of them in order for that to be true? Do they understand that salvation is free, but blessings and favor on the level they speak of cost something?* You see, there are grace blessings, which are the basic provisions any good parent would give to his or her child, things like food, clothing, and shelter—the basics, with no extra trimmings. But then there are *bonus* blessings. *Extra-dimensional* blessings. Blessings above and beyond the normal ration we all can claim as believers. God makes these blessings available to us.

At a price.

I don't know anyone who doesn't want to be blessed abundantly. Yet it seems to me that some of us just wait around with the attitude that God owes us something. Why is this? He already paid a debt He did not owe in order to purchase our salvation. Still, many of His children have a "Santa Claus" mentality: If we are good enough…if we wait long enough…plead loud enough…believe hard enough…blessings will miraculously rain down upon us from heaven.

I submit to you that we've missed the truth about what is really required of us in order to get those extra goodies. Are there really secrets to tapping into the reserve of God? Indeed there are! Does God really want to bless you? You'd better believe it! But God wants something from you, too. You say you want the favor of God on your life? Well you've got some home-work to do. In order to access His extra-dimensional blessings, you need to equip yourself with knowledge. You've got to find out who has the bless-ings you're looking for (that should be God), how to find Him, and what He requires from you in order to do something about your request. What are blessings? What is favor? And who has the key to the storehouse of these things? What motivates God to give us access to the things we desire? All these questions and more must be answered before we can enter into the abundant life that God wants for every believer.

SEEING IS BELIEVING

Speaking of believing, what do you believe? Your answer is important if you want to be blessed and highly favored.

> And without faith it is impossible to please God, because anyone who comes *to him* must believe that he exists and that he rewards those who earnestly *seek him.* (Hebrews 11:6)

Another translation says those who *diligently* seek Him. I'll assume—because you're reading this book—that you believe God exists, but do you believe God is really who He says He is? That He can really do what He says He can do? Do you believe that He really rewards those who seek Him? The "name it, claim it, and frame it" and the "confess it and possess it" schools of theology have caused many to focus their faith on the desired *object* or *result* in order to make their dreams come true. But I submit to you that the focus has been misplaced. Our gaze must be upon *Him,* the one who holds the key to the manifestation of all our dreams and desires. Do you believe that He is willing and able to fulfill His promises to you? To uphold every blessing He has promised in His Word? Only if you believe He is telling the truth will He be pleased with you. If you want a gift from the Giver, you must first be pleasing to Him. You must be someone He wants to give a gift to.

To be unsure whether God will keep His Word is to call Him a liar. Think about it. How does it make you feel when people behave as if they don't trust you to keep your promise to them? Their attitude doesn't exactly put you in the mood to do what you've said you'd do, does it? You think, *Well, forget it then. Why should I bother?* But you are happy to do anything for those who trust you completely. After all, these people are counting on you! You've got a standard to live up to. Their confidence might actually inspire you to push the envelope, to go the extra mile. You get a kick out of surprising them. It gives you pleasure to surpass their expectations. And so it is with God.

OH, CURSES!

In order for us to appreciate the full implication of a blessing, a comparison with curses is in order. God tells us in Deuteronomy 30:19 to *choose* blessings or curses. Now why would He tell us to choose if we didn't have a choice? And what exactly is a curse anyway? Besides the usual implication of profanity, my friend Webster says that a curse is misfortune that occurs when someone calls upon evil to bring harm or retribution to another. But I say that scriptural evidence points to *God's disregard* as the "curse" that allows us to fail when we rely on our own devices. What would cause us to be disregarded by God? Allowed by Him to fail? To struggle in the midst of unanswered prayer? The psalmist makes it clear:

> If I regard wickedness [iniquity] in my heart,
> The Lord will not hear;
> But certainly God has heard;
> He has given heed to the voice of my prayer.
> Blessed be God,

Who has not turned away my prayer,

Nor His lovingkindness from me. (Psalm 66:18-20,

NASB)

Two scriptures lead me to believe that iniquity is at least two steps beyond your garden-variety sin:

And the LORD passed by before him, and proclaimed, "The LORD, The LORD God, merciful and gracious, longsuffering, and abundant in goodness and truth, keeping mercy for thousands, forgiving iniquity and transgression and sin." (Exodus 34:6-7, KJV)

Seventy weeks are determined upon thy people and upon thy holy city, to finish the *transgression,* and to make an end of sins, and to make reconciliation for *iniquity.* (Daniel 9:24, KJV)

Sin is when you aim for the mark (righteousness) and miss it; transgression is when you acknowledge the mark but choose to do your own thing anyway. At both of these stages repentance is still readily in reach. But when iniquity sets in, repentance is harder to choose. Why? Because when you remove the standard, any sense of conviction goes out the window. After all, why should you repent for something that you don't believe is wrong? Based on my study, iniquity occurs when you decide the mark is not real or doesn't apply to you. You set your own standards. You declare, "Well, this is just the way I am—take it or leave it." Well, God chooses to leave it if your behavior doesn't line up with His Word. He will not partner with those who willfully disobey Him. He is far too holy for that. So He invites us to choose, to intentionally aim for His mark of righteousness. Do you want Him to be a participant and helper in your life, or do you want to strike out on your own? The choice is yours.

If you consider yourself a victim of generational curses, this concept might be hard for you to grasp. But again I say, why would God ask you to choose if you couldn't? The believer must understand that Jesus annihilated generational curses on the tree at Calvary. He became cursed in order to set us free from any curse that sought to claim us. What is now in effect are the consequences of patterns of generational *behavior.* Many of us adopt the less-than-victorious habits of our parents or grandparents because it seems like the "normal" thing to do, even though we reap the same disastrous results they did. That is not the hand of God smiting with a curse; that is simply the consequence of our unwise actions. On the other hand, through Christ we are free to have our lives transformed by the renewing of our minds (Romans 12:2). As our habits change, so does our harvest.

Even back in the Old Testament, God was quick to say that a curse would not alight on those who don't deserve it (Proverbs 26:2). He used Jeremiah and Ezekiel to tell the people to stop repeating the proverb that the children's teeth were on edge because their parents had eaten sour grapes (Jeremiah 31:29-30; Ezekiel 18:2-4). Each person, parent, or child, would be responsible for paying the penalty of his or her own sins. So there! You see, even back then, the scripture about God visiting the iniquity of the parents up to the fourth generation had been greatly misunderstood. His intention was not to bind people, but to halt the disintegration of society by not allowing self-destructive cycles to continue beyond the fourth generation. This explains the Israelites' cycle of repentance and disobedience throughout the Old Testament. Because of our right to choose, God had to set boundaries so we wouldn't permanently damage ourselves! This generational limitation became His way of stopping the madness, and He made the promise that He would love those who loved Him and hate those who hated him. So when the iniquities of your forefathers come to "visit" you, treat them like any other unwanted guest: Don't let them in!

Sometimes we are victims of others' sins because we find ourselves in the wrong place at the wrong time. In these cases we might say we are victims of circumstance but not curses. It is important to understand that we do indeed inherit genetic traits from our parents that predispose us to areas of weakness and strength (health and temperament-wise), but such predisposition is not God-imposed. Through God's power at work within us, we can claim victory over generational patterns, including health matters, as we remain attentive and obedient to the Holy Spirit's guidance in our everyday lives. A famous preacher tells of how he severed the chain binding him to his family's history of diabetes by changing the way he ate. Overcoming curses is not always that simple, but sometimes, after considering the ways of our parents and our parents' parents, we can effectively put our lives on a different path. It is just too easy to simply place the blame elsewhere instead of taking responsibility for our own lives. Remember this story?

> And His disciples asked Him, saying, "Rabbi, who sinned, this man or his parents, that he should be born blind?"
>
> Jesus answered, "It was neither that this man sinned, nor his parents; but it was in order that the works of God might be displayed in him." (John 9:2-3, NASB)

This man's misfortune was not anyone's fault. Through Jesus' eyes the situation looked completely different. Just as He described the death of Lazarus as mere sleep, Jesus saw the opportunity here to reverse an unfortunate natural circumstance and display God's power through the miracle of divine healing! God wants to demonstrate His power in our lives as well. So it is important to remember that misfortune and failure are not God's preference; therefore, He would never willingly cause the innocent to suffer for what someone else did. So much for curses.

THANK GOD FOR BLESSINGS!

What exactly is a blessing anyway? Well, Webster says that a blessing is the act of one who blesses. It is approval, encouragement, a thing conducive to happiness or welfare, or grace said at a meal. But to bless someone is to hold him or her in reverence, to hallow or consecrate by religious rite or word, to invoke divine care for or confer prosperity or happiness upon a person, or to protect and preserve him. While curses enable us to fail, blessings enable us to have success. That sounds good to me! I'll choose blessings over curses any day of the week!

We've been told to revere God, but did you ever stop to consider that God reveres *us?* He considers us an awesome creation of His hand. The angels are certainly still speechless as they consider the work of redemption that God was moved to do on our behalf. Sacrificing His own Son? How could we possibly be worth all of that, especially the way some of us behave? Yet God is fiercely passionate about us coming into the fullness of the inheritance He has set aside for us. He is not willing that any should perish. For this reason God is willing to allow the fullness of time to pass in order to redeem as many as possible. Let's face it, there must be times when He feels like pulling the plug on us when He witnesses some of the things that go on down here. But He doesn't.

Now that is grace to the utmost.

God gives us the promise of His divine care for us in spite of ourselves. He chooses to extend His riches and His joy to us in order to glorify Himself. Why? Not to gain our approval, but simply because He loves us. He wants to protect and preserve us until the day we meet in eternity and finally become one with Him. However, God is a practical God. He understands what it takes to live a good life in the natural sense, and He wants us to be fully equipped to live victoriously and abundantly. He does not treat us like unwanted stepchildren. He is a generous and benevolent Father who gains pleasure from blessing His children. Small wonder that David sought his Father's heart:

> I lift up my eyes to you,
>> to you whose throne is in heaven.
> As the eyes of slaves look to the hand of their master,
>> as the eyes of a maid look to the hand of her mistress,
> so our eyes look to the LORD our God,
>> till he shows us his mercy. (Psalm 123:1-2)

Well, what's God to do when it's put to Him like that? How could He let David down?

David was counting on Him completely, almost helplessly. No one with compassion can ignore another who so humbly states his case. Someone who is totally dependent upon and trusting in you. The now-famous prayer of Jabez also came from a heart that was totally reliant on the sovereign hand of God.

> Jabez cried out to the God of Israel, "Oh, that you
> would bless me and enlarge my territory! Let your
> hand be with me, and keep me from harm so that I will
> be free from pain." And God granted his request.
> (1 Chronicles 4:10)

Again, Jabez's belief that only the hand of God could accomplish what he needed moved the heart of God to answer Jabez's prayer.

Innumerable occasions and prayers throughout Scripture could be cited to prove this resounding point—God wants to bless us. He wants to prosper us. He wants to grant us divine protection. God wants to show up in our world and make His presence known to others by the things that He makes manifest in our lives. This is His desire for us individually, as well as corporately, as a body of worshipers. Our ability to be blessed affects kingdom business. He knows the world is looking for evidence of Him among His people. He longs to make us the envy of all who don't know Him in order to provoke them to seek relationship with Him.

Take a minute to consider how He had Moses bless the people in a most significant way as they headed through enemy territory toward the Promised Land:

> The Lord said to Moses, "Tell Aaron and his sons, 'This
> is how you are to bless the Israelites. Say to them:

> " ' "The LORD bless you
>   and keep you;
> the LORD make his face shine upon you
>   and be gracious to you;
> the LORD turn his face toward you
>   and give you peace." '
> "So they will put my name on the Israelites, and I will
>   bless them." (Numbers 6:22-27)

"The Lord bless you and keep you." But in order for Him to do that He must be looking at you. And when He looks at you He must be pleased. He must be inspired to be gracious to you. He has got to like what He sees. As long as He is looking at you, you can have the peace that surpasses all understanding. Because as long as He is looking at you, you can be sure that you are basking under the watchful eye of His protection. Oh, but when He looks away, the enemy of your soul can have a field day. He gets in his licks while God is not looking.

Now that doesn't mean that God doesn't see what's going on. It merely feels like it when He withdraws and declares, "I'm not touching that." He will only participate in what pleases Him—that is, when you're pressing toward the mark for the prize found in the high calling of Christ Jesus. But He becomes a sideline spectator when we dash down the field of life the wrong way, leaving plenty of room for Satan, our opponent, to tackle us.

So if blessings are all about having God's undivided attention, then surely favor is basking in the smile of God. Yes, when we make God smile, things happen! When we tickle the heart of God, He can't help Himself. He's got to show up and show out on your behalf! When God smiles, His favor flows toward us.

DO ME A FAVOR

What is *favor* exactly? As usual, my buddy Webster is ready with an answer. He profoundly states that a favor is friendly regard shown to another by a superior, approving consideration or attention, partiality, gracious kindness, leniency, effort in one's behalf or interest, attention, a token of love (usually worn conspicuously), or to do a kindness for, to treat gently or carefully, to give support or confirmation to, to afford advantages for success to—well, well, well! I don't know about you, but I am only that way with my friends. People I know. People I have walked with and talked with for a while. I've established a sense of trust with these people. We have bonded big time!

Don't you want God's tokens of love to be conspicuous in your life? Don't you want Him to afford advantages to you for your success? I most certainly do! But I also understand and dare to say that favors and the extent of their greatness are based entirely on the quality of the relationship. I may be telling too much of my business here, but I'm not too inclined to do a favor for just anybody unless the Holy Spirit prompts me. In today's culture you never know what you might be getting yourself into. Let's face it, if you were walking down the street and a stranger rushed up to you and said, "Do me a favor, loan me a hundred dollars right quick," you would look at them as if they were absolutely out of their mind. "I don't know you!" would probably be among your first words. But if a friend called you and made the same request, you probably wouldn't hesitate to hand it over if you could. After all, you know where your friend lives. But above and beyond that, you trust that person. Depending on the depth of your friendship, you might even give it without looking for it to be returned.

Well, God's got whatever it is that you need in the area of a favor. And

He is more than willing to give it to you if your relationship with Him is in the right place. Can He trust you? Have you been such a great friend that He would be moved to give to you abundantly? What type of friend is God looking for? What makes Him sit up and take notice of us? What makes Him say to us what He said to Moses?

> So the LORD said, "I have pardoned them according to
> your word." (Numbers 14:20, NASB)

Wow! You mean that we can influence God? Most definitely, if we are counted among His friends. John Wesley writes of Exodus 33:11, "And the Lord spake to Moses face to face as a man speaketh to his friend—which intimates not only that God revealed himself to Moses with greater clearness than to any other of the prophets, but also with greater expressions of particular kindness than to any other. He spake not as a king to a subject, but as a *man to his friend*, whom he loves, and with whom he takes sweet counsel."

What a glorious place to be! Intimate, exchanging ideas with God, reveling in the security that God is your friend. You are reconciled to Him through Jesus Christ, and now you have access to His throne. He anticipates your desires. You are free to make them known. He actually listens and does something about what you say if He's in agreement. And if He is not, well, you are such great friends that you don't mind being corrected by Him because you know that whatever He says is in your best interest. After all, He *does* know what is best, and *true* friends mirror one another's hearts and trust one another completely.

So what was it about those folks like Abraham, Moses, Joseph, David, and Daniel (just to name a few) that caught God's eye? What made them so special that He was moved to bless them so generously with wealth, prominent positions, and incredible legacies? What was it about Rahab, Ruth, Hannah, Abigail, the Shunnamite woman, the woman with the issue of blood, Esther, and Mary?

Mary!

Okay. Can we talk about Mary for a minute? Have you ever just put your hand on your hip and asked, "Why Mary? Why was Mary chosen to be the mother of Jesus?" If you're religious you've probably never wondered. But since I am slightly inclined to be nosy—just slightly—these are the sort of questions I ask. Of course, I don't have enough room to talk about all the people in the Bible that God gave the blessed-and-highly-favored nod to, so for the sake of the points I want to make in this book, I would like us to focus on Mary. After all, she is the one dubbed "blessed and highly favored" by Gabriel the angel. And since angels only repeat what God says, that indeed makes it official.

What was it about Mary that made God say, "I like her. I am going to grant her the blessing and favor that every single woman in Israel wants. Yep, she's the one to bear the Redeemer of Israel." Think about it. One day I heard someone musing: "If two football teams are playing against each other, and both are Christians, and both have prayed for God to help them win, how does He decide which team should get the victory?" Good question. One team will win and one will lose. Does it mean God likes the winning team better? Of course not. All determinations are made in accordance with God's kingdom purposes. When we are friends with God, we walk in the understanding that kingdom purposes should always take precedence over personal desires. The question is, Have we completely surrendered our personal desires to God? Do we trust His friendship enough to accept His determination and position on matters that concern us? When God selects someone to be a prominent player in the scheme of kingdom business, His selection is always based upon specific criteria.

That brings us back to Mary. I believe her conversation with Gabriel and her subsequent actions give us a lot of hints as to why God chose her to be "blessed among women." We can all take a clue from Mary and find ourselves also blessed. The blood of Jesus qualifies all of us to be friends with God, to expect His favor and His blessing upon our lives.

If we are willing to pay the price.

A TALE OF TWO CHILDREN

Consider the following scenario. In the center of this real-life drama is a father who has two children. One feels that the father owes him everything simply because he is a member of the family. This child does not pay much attention to the father. He merely calls or shows up when he needs something. He pouts and insults the father when he doesn't receive what he requested. The father, being a good father, does his paternal duty by supplying the basic necessities this child needs: food, provision, a home, help in time of trouble…you know—the bare essentials. Yet, this child always feels denied. This child will never feel blessed. This child has issues, issues that will grow like cancer if he does not deal with them by repenting. This child must ultimately make a true effort toward reconciliation in order to move the heart of his father.

On the other hand, this other child truly loves the father. This child is quite different. This child spends time with the father…does things to make the father happy…brings the father gifts…constantly showers the father with praise and love. This child brings a smile to the father's face.

For this child, the father always seeks extra ways to show him how much he appreciates and treasures their relationship. He gives this child extra gifts, takes note of the wishes uttered even in idle conversation. He wants this child to know that he is interested in everything concerning him.

Now don't get me wrong. The father loves both children, but one is selfish, the other selfless. There is something appealing about someone who has a giving spirit, someone who seeks to please and not to get. This kind of spirit is limitless in what it can do. It can also move hearts of stone. And if it can move hearts of stone, how much more can it move the heart of God, our heavenly Father?

Since we all come from a family, whether father or mother is present or absent, we can all relate to the situation I just described. Every family has one. Yeah, I'm talking about the favorite. But why is that person the favorite? In the midst of the seeming contest is always something that is clearly evident: One child curries the favor of the parent; another merely expects it. Expectations without actions are never enough.

Take Cain and Abel for instance. Abel gave God, his heavenly Father, a tithe or offering of the fatty cuts of meat from the first of his best lambs, so God looked on Abel and his offering with favor. Cain, on the other hand, gave God an offering he considered good enough, but it was not what God wanted. God had clearly established in the garden (after the fall of Adam and Eve) that a blood sacrifice was necessary for approaching him. So Abel honored God by bringing what He had asked for. But the produce Cain brought to God was not received because the ground was cursed. It was an unacceptable tithe, for it merely represented the fruit of his own efforts versus a heart that revered God's covenant. Cain became upset when God did not respond with favor to what he'd brought. When Cain's countenance displayed his resentment, God asked him a very profound question:

Why are you angry? Why is your face downcast? If
you do what is right, will you not be accepted? (Genesis
4:6-7)

Cain's actions clearly communicated his response. Instead of adjusting
his attitude and changing his approach to God, and instead of giving God
what He was looking for, Cain chose to blame Abel for his troubles: Cain
asked Abel to go out to the field with him, and there, Cain murdered him!
When confronted by God about his actions, Cain refused to confess or
repent. He felt his sin was justified, just as his father, Adam, did in the garden. As far as Cain was concerned, it was God's fault for choosing favorites;
never mind his own disobedience. For Cain, the consequences were not
pretty.

> The LORD said, "What have you done? Listen! Your
> brother's blood cries out to me from the ground. Now
> you are under a curse and driven from the ground,
> which opened its mouth to receive your brother's blood
> from your hand. When you work the ground, it will no
> longer yield its crops for you. You will be a restless wan-
> derer on the earth."
>
> Cain said to the LORD, "My punishment is more
> than I can bear. Today you are driving me from the
> land, and I will be hidden from your presence; I will
> be a restless wanderer on the earth, and whoever finds
> me will kill me."
>
> But the LORD said to him, "Not so; if anyone kills
> Cain, he will suffer vengeance seven times over." Then

the LORD put a mark on Cain so that no one who found
him would kill him. So Cain went out from the LORD's
presence and lived in the land of Nod, east of Eden.
(Genesis 4:10-16)

There you have it. When we justify our stubbornness, we end up being
shocked by the magnitude of the consequences—although we shouldn't
be. Perhaps we hope against hope that we will somehow escape the reper-
cussions of our actions. Or we think that if God is a God of compassion
then surely He will let us slide this time. But this issue has nothing to do
with His compassion and everything to do with our obedience. Whether it
is obedience in tithing or obedience in another area, we cannot expect to
be blessed if we are not willing to do what is required of us by God. You
see, when God withdraws his regard, failure is enabled only to be followed
shortly by our heart's true desires going unfulfilled.

Even Cain understood the weighty implications of being separated
from God. But God, ever the responsible Father, assured Cain that he
would still have His protection and basic blessings of necessity, but without
any fancy perks. No extra rewards. Yet it all would have been so simple. If
only Cain had turned to Abel and said, "Hey, where did you get that
unblemished, fatted lamb? Where can I get one?" If only Cain had dealt
with his shortcomings, repented, and given God what He wanted, the story
could have had a drastically different ending. If only…

The story of Cain and Abel rings true in too many modern day lives.
Many of us want the favor and extra-dimensional blessings of God, but we
are unwilling to go the extra mile or pay the price required to gain them.
Instead when we observe others being blessed, we become disgruntled
and discount the steps they took to get the blessing. Or worse yet, we

accuse God of being unfair—which means that we still haven't dealt with ourselves and the part we played or didn't play in our own disappointment. Many of us chafe at, or completely disregard, God's instructions for tithing, righteous living, and covenant relationships, then wonder why we are unable to reach the realm of higher blessing and favor. The truth of the matter is this: Based on our own disobedience, known or unknown, we are simply not in the right position to receive.

This point was brought home to me by a recent experience. A friend of mine and I were comparing the features on our Palm Pilots. I decided that I wanted one of the programs he had on his, so he prepared to download it by beaming it to my Palm. We had our units face each another, and he hit the appropriate button. His unit flashed the message "searching…searching…searching…" My unit flashed the message, "waiting for sender…waiting for sender…waiting for sender…" After a while he grew impatient and moved. My unit flashed the message: "Connection has been broken." To help figure out why the transfer didn't work, I tried to beam his Palm. As soon as I hit the appropriate button, the message flashed "Searching…" His unit displayed "Waiting for sender…" Meanwhile another friend present asked if I had everything turned on correctly. I insisted, "Of course!" But at that same moment my unit flashed, "Your option to beam has been turned off. Would you like to turn it on?" Well! After recovering from my surprise, I pressed "yes," and the transfer of data to his Palm was successfully accomplished. However, I was never able to receive a program from him. When I got home I examined my user manual to learn how to solve our beaming problem and discovered that we were holding our units in the wrong position.

What's the point? God is searching…searching…searching for someone to give a blessing to. He really does want to bless us and give us in-

credible gifts! Meanwhile we are waiting…waiting…waiting…for a blessing. Sometimes while God is preparing to download a blessing to us, our
impatience causes us to move, and the connection is broken. Other times
we are not in the right position to receive what He has for us. He said, "My
people are destroyed for lack of knowledge" (Hosea 4:6). Some of us think
we're open to receive from God, but our option to receive may have been
turned off by our disobedience. That disobedience separates us from Him
and damages the line of communication needed to secure the blessing. Of
course, we don't always deliberately cause a disconnection. Many of us have
just not checked the manual—God's Word—to obtain the knowledge about
how this blessing thing works and about how to get in the right position.

Somebody reading this is now thinking, *Well where does God's grace
come into all of this?* I'll tell you where:

> For *by grace* are ye saved through faith; and that not of
> yourselves: it is the gift of God: Not of works, lest any
> man should boast. (Ephesians 2:8, KJV)

You have already been given an extraordinary free gift that you did not
deserve. Getting hold of the extras is up to you. Don't confuse sovereign
acts of God with free blessings. There is a big difference. Remember extra-
dimensional blessings minus our human devices are called miracles.

TIME TO CHOOSE

Have you simply been expecting God to bless you and now are wondering
why nothing has been happening? Or maybe you've experienced a little

taste of the blessed life and you long for more. Well, today is your day. We are about to cross the great divide, to switch from black and white to living color, from mediocre to incredible, from merely existing to really living, living in the fullness of what God desires for all of His children because He loves us so.

We are going to take it up a notch, stage a revolution in the spirit, and step into the extra-dimensionally blessed life. The highly favored life. Ah yes, it's a wonderful life! It can be your life when you link your faith to actions. Remember: Faith without works is dead, dead, dead! Don't just sit around waiting for God to bless you and complain under your breath when everything remains the same. Stop simply expecting and start pulling on heaven's windows and doors. Start tapping into the heart of God and currying favor from His hand.

Did you know being blessed is up to you? Mm-hm, it's true. God has left it up to you to determine whether you will be in a position to be blessed.

> This day I call heaven and earth as witnesses against you
> that I have set before you *life* and death, blessings and
> curses. Now *choose life*. (Deuteronomy 30:19)

Choose blessings! God is in the blessing business, but you've got to be standing in the right spot. I don't know anyone who would deliberately choose curses and death, yet many do so out of ignorance. It is time to be illuminated so you can make the right choices. To learn valuable lessons from those who attained the blessed and favored life in order to imitate them and gain the same, or even greater, results. I think I've chatted this up enough. Let's get down to the meat of the matter—how to be blessed and highly favored. As I mentioned earlier, to coin the title of a popular movie, there's something about Mary, and we're about to find out exactly what it is.

Thoughts to Ponder

- Is God your friend or just an acquaintance?
- Do you really know Him? Does He know you?
- How would you describe your friendship with God?
- Do you think God owes you? Do you curry his favor or are you merely expecting it?
- Are you doing things that make God want to turn His face away from you, or do you make Him smile?
- What can you do to improve your relationship with God?

the issue of purity

LIVING FOR THE ONE YOU BELONG TO

In the sixth month, God sent the angel Gabriel to
Nazareth, a town in Galilee, to a virgin pledged to
be married to a man named Joseph, a descendant of
David. The virgin's name was Mary.

LUKE 1:26-27

Don't you find it interesting that the first thing the Bible tells us about
Mary is where she lived and that she was a virgin? Oh, I can hear the collective groan already: Gee, we were having a good time. Why'd you have to
go and spoil the mood by bringing up virginity and purity?

When I was a kid I decided I would eat my vegetables first and get
them out of the way so I could enjoy the rest of my meal. I hated vegetables! As long as I could see them sitting there next to my sweet potatoes,
they just took the joy out of my eating experience. I think sometimes
we view lessons on holiness and purity just as we do those vegetables. The
topic makes us nervous. It just takes all the joy out of the service because
suddenly we are forced to face something that we do not like—the fact

that not one of us is perfect. "As it is written: 'There is no one righteous, not even one'" (Romans 3:10).

That's why God's mercies are new every morning. His grace is eternally permanent, but when we open our eyes every morning, He pours out fresh mercy because He already knows that somewhere along the way we're going to need it. We are going to mess up in thought, word, or deed before the day is over, and His mercy is ready and waiting to meet the occasion. What a loving Father! God anticipates our failures and has a ready-made solution for our problems. His mercy is there to equip us to continue in His grace. It is there to help us have the strength to lay aside the things that so easily beset us and finally get the victory. He is rooting for us to make it.

Those fresh mercies are like a welcome glass of cool water. When we falter in the race or completely fall down, God is standing there, holding the water to our lips, inviting us to take a long swig. "Come on," He says, "don't give up now. You can do it. My grace is sufficient for you. Take a drink of My mercy, refresh yourself and keep going." He is our greatest cheerleader. And our greatest helper. It is only by His spirit that we can be what He longs for us to be: whole and holy in His sight. Holiness is important to God. Why? Because we were made to reflect His image to the world, and God is, first and foremost, holy.

FIRST THINGS FIRST

I believe that when the Holy Ghost inspired men to write the Word of God, He didn't mince words. No, no. He dictated what was on His mind and made it plain what was of utmost importance to Him. Every word was deliberately placed, in precise order, for His point to ring loud and true.

26

The first thing God says about Mary is that she lived in Nazareth and she was a virgin.

You know how people are when you ask about a young lady. They usually say, "Oh, she's a nice girl!" Well, God went beyond obvious externals to the intimate details. Mary was a virgin. She had kept herself pure. She had kept herself separate, awaiting a promise. She was pledged to be married to Joseph, a descendant of the house of David.

We, too, are pledged to be married. We are the collective bride of Christ. He looks forward to His wedding day with great anticipation. Until then, His hope is that we will keep ourselves pure for Him, that we will keep ourselves separate from the things that court our flesh. He hopes we will conduct ourselves as a good fiancée should, doing nothing to stir up the jealousy of the One she loves. To stir up His jealousy is to offend Him. Offense will separate us from Him, inhibit our intimacy, and sour the courtship.

Trust me, no one feels like sending flowers and giving gifts when the courtship is shaky.

It's safe to say that one reason Mary kept herself separate was because she was aware she was promised to another. Are you walking in the awareness that you are promised to another? That you are promised to Christ? Most of us do not usually keep this thought at the front of our minds. It is hard to be mindful of One whom you cannot see. It is even harder to think of being promised to One with whom you've never had physical contact. Yet, whether married or single, we have been spoken for by a heavenly Lover—our match made by a heavenly Father. We are to walk as if we belong to Someone in honor of that promise.

One night I had a dream that I was in a place where I.D. cards were required. Everyone had one but me. After ransacking my purse and other belongings in an effort to find my own, I came up empty-handed. I felt out of place with no way to verify my identity, so I decided to play the whole thing off by pretending I had just misplaced my I.D.

"I don't know where my I.D. card is," I said. "My husband must have it."

"Your husband?" someone said. "You don't have a husband."

"Yes, I do," I countered defensively, embarrassed that someone was on to me and knew I was single.

"What is his name?" the person asked, narrowing her eyes. I paused. I was stuck, about to be completely uncovered, when a thought struck me. My eyes brightened, and a smile slowly spread across my face.

"J. C. Lord," I said with emphasis on each letter and word. (Jesus Christ Lord—get it?) Then, as the realization of what that meant really hit me, I straightened up in full confidence and announced once again, "Yes, that's right. J. C. Lord. I'm Mrs. Lord!" I could no longer contain my mirth. A giggle escaped my lips as I looked at the stupefied expression of my interrogator.

I awoke still chuckling. "Wow, Lord," I said. "So many times I forget that my identity is really hidden in You, that I am Your beloved and intended. Thank You for reminding me." I found myself reveling in that knowledge for the rest of the day. What a difference it made in my attitude to know that I was promised to and possessed by One so great.

FILL 'ER UP!

When you meet someone who is engaged, you may be struck by the fact that his or her entire existence is geared toward the wedding day—saving money for the wedding, dieting, working out, preparing that body for the honeymoon night. Everything is focused on being one's best for the big day and the days to follow. The flirtations and invitations of members of the opposite sex could just as well be water rolling off the back of a duck; engaged people have eyes and ears only for their intended. They are just not interested in anything or anyone who would distract them from getting to the church on time. Their lamps are full, so to speak.

But those who don't focus on the reality of one day seeing Christ and uniting with Him are like the foolish virgins in Matthew 25 who fell asleep on the job. Unprepared for the journey and weary of waiting for the groom, they awoke with a start to find themselves lacking the oil they needed to get to the wedding feast. The virgins who were serious about getting to the wedding had enough. They were prepared to go the distance. In the face of those who were not, their attitude was: "Hey, it's every woman for herself. Sorry. Can't help you. See ya, wouldn't wanna be ya!" When the groom finally arrived, the women who were not ready were left behind.

And so it is with us. It is up to us individually to arrive at the wedding. No one else will be able to help us get there. How seriously do you take your wedding day with Christ? Something is required of us now in order to see Him then, at the wedding feast. And that is merely the beginning of what is required in order to receive the blessings He wants to bestow on your life.

> Who may ascend the hill of the LORD?
>> Who may stand in his holy place?
> He who has *clean hands and a pure heart,*
>> who does not lift up his soul to an idol
>> or swear by what is false.
> *He will receive blessing from the LORD*
>> *and vindication from God his Savior.* (Psalm 24:3-5)

> Surely God is good to Israel,
>> to those who are *pure* in heart. (Psalm 73:1)

> Blessed are the *pure* in heart,
>> for they will see God. (Matthew 5:8)

Who are the pure in heart? Those who do not delight in or serve the works of the flesh but instead walk after the mandates of the Spirit. Those who do not harbor unforgiveness, sexual immorality, impurity, anger, hatred, jealousy, envy, idolatry, selfishness, and the like. We've got to take out the trash, so to speak, and get rid of the things that God considers filthy. In order to be blessed we must purify our hearts and our hands. We must put ourselves in the position to see God. To be pleasing in His sight. The extra-dimensional blessings abide in His presence. We gain access to them when we remove everything from our lives that separates us from Him. We must roll up our sleeves and be willing to do the work of repentance.

Mary was pure in heart. Her actions reflected this. She set herself apart. And God showed up in her personal world and blessed her. Many will say as they slide across the grace of God, "Well, God knows my heart." He sure does, and it doesn't take a lot of guesswork to figure out the attitudes and beliefs we harbor.

> How can you who are evil say anything good? For out of the overflow of the *heart* the mouth speaks. The good man brings good things out of the good stored up in him, and the evil man brings evil things out of the evil stored up in him. (Matthew 12:34-35)

God is not moved by our good intentions; He is moved by our obedience to Him. As far as God is concerned, what you say and do reflects what is going on in your heart. And though He loves us enough to invite us to come as we are, He loves us too much to leave us in our former condition. He wants to be in fellowship with us, yet He cannot stand the stench of sin. Have you ever been trapped in a close space with someone who had bad body odor? It's enough to make you pass out. You can't wait to get out of that person's presence. That's how God feels about being near us in our sinfulness. Therefore, He wants us to clean up our acts. That is why He hands us the Grace soap and a Mercy sponge and tells us to get busy!

> Let us draw near to God with a sincere heart in full assurance of faith, having our *hearts* sprinkled to *cleanse* us from a guilty conscience and having our bodies washed with pure water. (Hebrews 10:22)

> Come near to God and he will come near to you. Wash your hands, you sinners, and purify your *hearts,* you double-minded. (James 4:8)

Why is it so important that you embrace purity? Because it is the portal through which you must step to get to the blessed life! Small wonder the psalmist said, "If I had cherished sin in my heart, the Lord would not have listened" (Psalm 66:18). He knew he must first be what God wanted him to be before God would do what he wanted. To ask God to bless us when we do not honor His Word by living obedient lives is to ask Him to compromise His very nature. God cannot go against His own Word. He cannot reward disobedience or avert the consequences of our actions. God gave us His commandments—and there are more than ten—for our protection. They arose out of His love for us because He wanted to help us avoid loss, heartache, and bodily harm. God saw that certain reactions or consequences would accompany certain actions, and He deemed for the sake of those He cherished—us—that those actions should be avoided. He took the time to point out through Moses that if Israel did A, B would occur. But if they didn't do A, they would reap a less desirable result. Therefore, He said, *"Choose."* As I said before, you have a big say-so in how blessed you will be based upon the way you choose to live.

> If you fully obey the LORD your God and carefully follow all his commands I give you today, the LORD your God will set you high above all the nations on earth. All these blessings will come upon you and accompany you if you obey the LORD your God....However, if you do not obey the LORD your God and do not carefully follow all his commands and decrees I am giving you today, all these curses will come upon you and overtake you. (Deuteronomy 28:1-2,15)

So there it is. We either worship God in spirit and walk out the truth of His commands, or we suffer the consequences of our sinful ways. I suggest you read Deuteronomy 28 for yourself, examine your options, and then joyfully choose life and blessings.

> Blessed are all who fear the LORD,
> who walk in his ways.

You will eat the fruit of your labor;

blessings and prosperity will be yours. (Psalm 128:1-2)

You come to the help of those who *gladly do right,*

who remember your ways. (Isaiah 64:5)

Basically God is saying, "Hey, all I'm asking for is some respect and a heart that rejoices in being obedient to Me. Walk in reverence. Though I'm the friend who sticks closer than a brother, don't treat Me like a common buddy. I am God. Recognize the difference and conduct yourself accordingly. Don't be obedient to Me out of duty, being grudgingly religious and unpleasant. I would rather you joyfully fulfill my wishes because you love Me and sincerely want to make Me happy." That's not too much to ask, especially when we consider all He has done and all He has promised us.

THE BEST OF COMPANIONS

But perhaps this is where we miss it. We make costly mistakes because we lack knowledge. People don't deliberately choose to rob themselves of a blessing. This is why you must fill yourself with the knowledge of God's Word. Know what your heavenly Father likes and doesn't like, what your spiritual rights are. Satan takes advantage of what you don't know. He knows God's Word inside out, and he knows how to twist it in the hearts of those who are not soundly rooted in the knowledge of what God has to say about how to live.

How you live your life is based not only on *what* you know, but also on the influence of *whom* you know and with whom you choose to align yourself. Our companions can affect our ability to stay pure. Mary was pledged to be married to Joseph, a descendant of the house of David. He came from good stock. He was a member of the family of God. His lineage held a precious promise from the Lord. God had promised David that the throne would not depart from his family line. Joseph was the next man up. Therefore, in perfect accordance with what God had pledged to David, Joseph was chosen to be the earthly father of the King of kings and Lord of lords. The people God places in our lives promote His kingdom design. But those we choose for ourselves can pull us off course by influencing us to listen to the voice of the flesh and the voices in the world that attempt to drown out the voice of the Holy Spirit.

The effect of being near sin is a lot like what happens when you're near people who smoke. Nonsmokers who spend any time in a smoke-filled room complain of smelling like an ashtray afterward. The smoke of others saturates their clothing, their hair, their skin. If you didn't know better, you would think they themselves had been smoking! I once lived in an apartment previously occupied by a smoker. Though the carpet had been cleaned many times, on sunny days when the temperature rose, the smell of smoke also rose and filled the room. Sin is that way. Though you yourself may not partake of the things your associates do, the smell of their deeds will cling to you. It will begin to penetrate your spirit and, ever so slowly, your attitude will become more and more like theirs. Solomon was a wise man until he surrounded himself with wives who worshiped idols. They eventually seduced him away from the God who had blessed him so extravagantly. We cannot avoid everybody in the world, but we can more carefully pick our circle of Christian friends.

> Don't you know that a little yeast works through the
> whole batch of dough? Get rid of the old yeast that you

may be a new batch without yeast—as you really are. For Christ, our Passover lamb, has been sacrificed. Therefore let us keep the Festival, not with the old yeast, the yeast of malice and wickedness, but with bread without yeast, the bread of sincerity and truth.

I have written you in my letter not to associate with sexually immoral people—not at all meaning the people of this world who are immoral, or the greedy and swindlers, or idolaters. In that case you would have to leave this world. But now I am writing you that you must not associate with anyone who calls himself a brother but is sexually immoral or greedy, an idolater or a slanderer, a drunkard or a swindler. With such a man *do not even eat.* (1 Corinthians 5:6-11)

Paul's words are seemingly harsh, but he knew that "evil companions corrupt good manners." Or, as Proverbs 12:26 tells us, the way of the wicked leads the righteous man astray. Why did Paul say not to eat with such people? Because eating is a communion of sorts. It is the place where we relax. When we relax we become vulnerable, open to whatever is said or done. We cannot afford to relax in a world where the enemy of our souls is ever relentlessly on the prowl, like a lion, seeking whom he may devour. We must be ever alert.

Perhaps this is what Daniel and the Hebrew boys Shadrach, Meshach, and Abednego understood. Perhaps this is why they refused to eat the meats and sweets from the king's table. They chose to stick to the diet God had prescribed in His law. The difference between them and those who ate whatever they were served was clearly apparent—they were found to be in better health and far wiser than the others in the court. No doubt those who ate whatever they were served were quite sluggish from all their indulgent feasting. Daniel, along with Shadrach, Meshach, and Abednego, was blessed with a prominent position in the king's court that lasted through several different administrations. We never hear anymore about those who pigged out—no pun intended.

WATCHING YOUR DIET

We cannot eat what the world eats and expect to be spiritually healthy. Indeed, what we feed the most will be the strongest. This is why the knowledge of God's Word is of the utmost importance. It is our only standard and foundation for godly living. Our spirit must be stronger than our flesh in order for us to live a pure and consecrated life before God. We must make sure that although we live in the world, we are not *of* the world. Jesus was so balanced in this. He understood that He had to eat physically, but His more crucial diet was a spiritual one. When assaulted by temptation He knew what God had said, and His Father's Word kept Him rooted in his faith.

> Jesus answered [Satan], "It is written: 'Man does not live on *bread alone,* but on every word that comes from the mouth of God.'" (Matthew 4:4)

Jesus walked among those in the world, ministered to them, and pointed them toward an eternal mind-set. Then He withdrew to spend His vulnerable time with His Father and those who were seeking God. He built Himself up with His Father's words and made decisions based only upon His Father's advice. He did not listen to those who offered contrary suggestions. He ate the Word of God. He digested it and lived it. And He surrounded Himself with an inner circle of those who were striving to do the same.

I am convinced that godly companions also surrounded Mary. Her fiancé was a godly man who was able to hear and follow God. Her cousin Elizabeth was a godly woman who was able to believe God for her own miracle—a child in her old age, a very special child, John the Baptist, who would pave the way for Jesus Christ.

When you want to be successful, you should hang around successful people. Always take advice from those who have excelled at what you your-self are striving to do. If you want to live a holy life, then associate with those who are walking in the same direction. Be transparent and allow them to hold you accountable to the standard God sets before you.

Mary spent time with Elizabeth and received a confirmation that, yes, she was on the right path. That visitation from the angel was not a figment of her imagination—it was real. It was of God. Elizabeth had to have been a tremendous support to Mary as she faced this momentous event. Let's face it: She couldn't tell just anybody about her circumstances. Who would under-stand it?! *Pregnant by the Spirit of God? Come on, who are you trying to fool?* Her situation could have been made a mess if shared with the wrong person, namely, someone who wasn't walking in the Spirit. I'm sure Elizabeth coun-seled Mary on how to conduct herself until God had set all the pieces and players in place. Godly counsel is crucial to maintaining purity and faith in a world that constantly pulls at our flesh and our fears. If we're honest, it is our unbelief and fear that cause us to fall, to give in to moments of immediate gratification while ignoring the eternal ramifications.

Now, a lot of single women are probably struggling through this chapter. You are saying, "Michelle, I am not a virgin. Does that mean that God will not bless me? I've blown it. How can I salvage what has been lost?" I have good news for you. Through the blood of Jesus your virginity has been spiritually restored.

> If anyone is in Christ, he is a *new* creation; the old has
> gone, the *new* has come! (2 Corinthians 5:17)

There is no need to wallow in mourning or to fall into self-condemnation. You are not alone in your struggles with the flesh. God is well aware that we are but dust. This is why He made a provision for our restoration.

Even David, the king of Israel who had an adulterous affair and committed murder to cover it up, was still called "a man after God's own heart." Certainly he was not perfect, but he was repentant. He confessed his sin (remember, confession goes beyond *admitting* what you did to saying what *God* says about what you did), accepted the consequences, submitted himself to the correction and chastening of the Lord, and did not repeat that offense again. Though he was a mighty warrior and king of a powerful nation, the only thing that truly mattered to him was the presence of God in his life. He could not stand the thought of facing another day without God. He did not consider himself too high to call out to the Lord.

> Cleanse me with hyssop, and I will be clean;
> wash me, and I will be whiter than snow....
> Hide your face from my sins
> and blot out all my iniquity.

Create in me a pure heart, O God,

and renew a steadfast spirit within me.

Do not cast me from your presence

or take your Holy Spirit from me.

Restore to me the joy of your salvation

and grant me a willing spirit, to sustain me....

You do not delight in sacrifice, or I would bring it;

you do not take pleasure in burnt offerings.

The sacrifices of God are a broken spirit;

a broken and contrite heart,

O God, you will not despise.

(Psalm 51:7,9-12,16-17)

David cried out to God, and the Lord heard him. Your repentance and your cry for forgiveness have been heard by God. God has thrown your sins as far as the east is from the west to be remembered no more. He has granted you a fresh start. A new beginning. A chance to get it right this time.

Don't get hung up on the terminology of virginity. Embrace the principle of purity from the inside out: A pure heart that leads to pure actions, actions that get the attention of God and please Him. Yes, Mary was a virgin physically, and some of us are not. But Mary had something that we all can have—a clean heart and a right spirit. You see, the issue is not really physical virginity, it's spiritual chastity. Living a pure life. A godly life. The bottom line is that Mary did not offend God. This should be our daily goal. Remember, if you want to be blessed by someone, do not offend him or her.

Thoughts to Ponder

- Are you walking in the awareness that you are promised to someone?
- How is your courtship with God going?
- If someone "smelled" you, would that person smell the smoke of the world or the fragrance of the Holy Spirit?
- Take inventory of those who form your inner circle of friends. Do they influence your spirit or your flesh? Which influence is strongest at this time?
- What spiritual food are you eating? What things in your diet need to change?

THREE

the heart of the father

GRASPING WHAT GETS GOD'S ATTENTION

The angel went to [Mary] and said, "Greetings, you
who are highly favored! The Lord is with you."

LUKE 1:28

What a powerful phrase! "The Lord is with you!" Can you imagine how
Mary felt?

E.V. Hill, one of the most respected preachers of our time, once
preached a sermon in which he recounted an international trip he took
with Jesse Jackson. Since Rev. Jackson was the celebrated guest on this
excursion, all deference and protection was afforded to him. At times, as
they went from place to place, the pastor and the statesman would be separated in the bustle of the crowd. As Pastor Hill tried to make his way back
to the side of Rev. Jackson, security guards would circumvent his efforts
until he said, "I'm with him." All the special treatment he received on the
journey was because of his affiliation with the guest of honor. All entrées he
enjoyed were because of his association with Rev. Jackson.

Pastor Hill concluded his sermon by saying that one day we would
stand before the pearly gates of heaven. And as we head toward the open

gate an angel will block our path. But because of Jesus we will be able to point toward the throne room where God resides and say, "I'm with Him." And on that declaration the angel will step aside and allow us into that great heavenly city. Well, I have to tell you I just shouted. It was such an incredible picture of what our association with the Lord really means.

LET US DRAW NEAR

The Lord was with Mary. And, oh, how we need His presence in our lives as well in order to be blessed! He is our entrée into the blessed and highly favored life. With Him as our escort we are blessed going in and blessed going out. Blessed when we sit and blessed when we rise. Which means we must invite Him into our midst. I've never seen a person willfully hang out uninvited with someone for very long. No one who understands their own worth would force himself or herself on an unwilling companion. Why go where you are tolerated when you can be celebrated somewhere else? God is a gentleman. He doesn't force Himself on anyone; He politely waits for an invitation to be a part of your life. He doesn't pry into your affairs. He waits for you to open the door.

> Come near to *God* and he will come near to you.
> (James 4:8)

> Here I am! I *stand* at the *door* and *knock.* If anyone hears
> my voice and opens the *door,* I will come in and eat with
> him, and he with me. (Revelation 3:20)

God has perfect etiquette. He will enter the parlor of your heart and abide there only by invitation. Obviously Mary had extended the invitation and the Lord had taken her up on it. Not only had she invited Him into her life, she celebrated His presence. Mary was a worshiper. She was being rewarded for diligently seeking the Lord. She worshiped God in spirit and in truth.

What does it mean to really worship God in spirit and in truth? Worshiping God goes beyond the worship service on Sunday morning. Worship is the rehearsing of God's Word continually. Meditating on it and living it twenty-four hours a day, seven days a week, three hundred sixty-five days a year. Worship is constant surrender to the Lord and living in agreement with His Word. That's right, talking the talk and walking the walk. Being living epistles for all to see. Our worship of God should affect our countenance, attitude, and actions. Worship is continually saying yes to God in every area of our lives.

Worship involves loving the unlovely, overlooking offenses, refusing to tell off someone who deserves it. Submitting to a difficult boss, to an even more difficult mate. Being kind to a hateful coworker. Blessing that driver who deliberately cut you off in traffic. Giving when you feel you don't really have it to give. Every occasion that you say yes to God and no to your natural inclinations, you are worshiping. Worship is maintaining an attitude of humility even when you have every right to feel proud. It is recognizing that all you have and all you are come from the hand of God. Now *that* is worship. Mary flowed in her worship. It bubbled up from her inner self like a fountain. It touched others. It was contagious to those around her. They were moved to praise God as well.

When Elizabeth heard Mary's greeting, the baby leaped in her womb, and Elizabeth was filled with the Holy Spirit. In a loud voice she exclaimed: "Blessed are you among women, and blessed is the child you will bear! But why am I so favored, that the mother of my Lord should come to me? As soon as the sound of your greeting reached my ears, the baby in my womb leaped for joy." (Luke 1:41-44)

When you are a true worshiper, you affect people around you. They recognize the hand of God on your life. When you are a worshiper nothing is a coincidence, everything is a miracle, and you are quick to give the glory back to God. Mary knew the source of her blessings and loudly proclaimed it.

> My soul glorifies the Lord,
>   and my spirit rejoices in God my Savior,
> for he has been mindful
>   of the humble state of his servant.
> From now on all generations will call me blessed,
>   for the Mighty One has done great things for me—
>   holy is his name.
> His mercy extends to those who fear him, from generation to generation. (Luke 1:46-50)

There was no claiming credit or leaving the conclusion to chance in Mary's proclamation. She understood that those who fear the Lord receive His mercy and that those who worship God receive a measure of blessings and favor above what can be measured or anticipated.

WHEN THE PRAISES GO UP

What is it about worship and praise? When the praises go up, the blessings come down, as the popular saying goes. Let's think about this. Don't you love being around those who have good things to say about you? You like those people, don't you? Why? Because they like you! Well, God loves to visit with those who love Him. However, praise is just the beginning for Him.

> Know therefore that the LORD your God is God; he is the faithful God, keeping his covenant of *love* to a thousand generations of *those* who *love* him and keep his commands. (Deuteronomy 7:9)

> Then I said: "O LORD, God of heaven, the great and awesome God, who keeps his covenant of *love* with *those* who *love* him and obey his commands." (Nehemiah 1:5)

Notice that loving Him and obeying Him are never separate in the Lord's eyes. He visits those who couple their praise with a worshipful, obedient life. God showed up for those whose hands and hearts were clean, for those whose lips acknowledged Him with the praise that is due Him. He showed up for those who truly wanted to see and to know Him. When Moses went into the Tent of Meetings to worship, God would come down. His presence would cover and fill the tent to overflowing. Those standing far off could see the glory of God from where they were. It was an awesome sight. God showed up for Moses so that the people of Israel would know that He had Moses' back, and they were to do as Moses instructed them. When God has your back, there should be no question about it to others around you.

Remember when Moses came down from the mountain after receiving the commandments and after spending time in the presence of God? His face was shining so brilliantly that the people had to step back. They couldn't look at him; they needed sunglasses! He had to cover his face with a veil. Your encounters with God should also be evident on your countenance. The evidence should be clear that He shows up in your daily life and in the circumstances you encounter.

OH, THE GLORY!

When Solomon dedicated the temple he had built to the Lord, everyone had assembled to worship Him. The priests had gathered to do service unto the Lord, the ark of the covenant had been set in its right place in the Holy of Holies, and then an awesome thing happened. As Solomon invited God to come and reside in this place built for Him, the glory of the Lord came down and filled the temple. It was so intense, so glorious, that no one could remain in the temple. The priests could not perform their duties, so overtaken were they by the presence of God! That is what praise and worship does.

> When Solomon finished praying, fire came down from heaven and consumed the burnt offering and the sacrifices, and the *glory* of the LORD *filled* the temple. The priests could not enter the temple of the LORD because the *glory* of the LORD *filled* it. (2 Chronicles 7:1-2)

God comes down and dwells in the midst of our praise, in the midst of our righteous living. It pleases Him to take up residence in a worshipful life. It is important to note that a few specific actions prompted God's powerful visitation and instruction. Let's take a look.

First, a temple had been prepared for God. Your body is the temple of the Holy Spirit. Have you prepared your temple to receive Him? Is it a place He would like to enter and abide?

Next, the ark of the covenant was put in its place. Is your covenant with God intact? Solomon prayed a prayer of dedication to the Lord, acknowledging His full ownership of the temple. Have you completely dedicated your life, your love, your all to Him? Do you love God with all your heart, all your soul, all your mind, and all your strength? Does your temple really belong to Him? Covenant is a serious matter to God, a matter of life and death. When God sealed His vow to Abraham, He walked between the separated halves of a dead animal, a gesture that meant, in essence, if I do not keep my promise let me be as this animal is—dead and cut off even from itself (Genesis 15:9-21).

Then sacrifices and burnt offerings were rendered unto the Lord. Is your life all about you, or are you willing to sacrifice the desires of your flesh to obey the Word of the Lord? God prefers cheerful obedience over sacrifice. It delights His heart when He knows that we are happy to be obedient to Him, not out of religious duty but to honor our relationship with Him. Religious people are not happy people. They are unpleasant because they find no joy in what they do. They are motivated by the letter of the law, which kills. I encourage you to be motivated to obedience by love. The spirit of love will give life to your relationship with God and joy to your heart.

When all these things are in place, a miraculous thing occurs: God's glory fills your life. His presence so saturates you that it pushes some things out to make room for Him and for all that He wants to accomplish in your life. Remember those priests who couldn't go into the temple to perform their duties? The Spirit of God had overcome them, leaving no room for human effort, no room for manipulations to drum up the presence of God. No, God was taking over. He showed up and showed out—He performed extraordinarily! There was no disputing His awesome presence that day; it was clearly apparent to all in attendance. Nothing else needed to be said or done. No pleas or requests needed to be voiced. Thoughts of lack or difficulty were banished when God visited. And that's what He still does! When He comes onto the scene, everything we want, need, or are looking and longing for comes with Him.

JESUS IN THE HOUSE

I was recently at a church where the congregants were encouraged to call out for money. There they were, calling money to themselves like calling a puppy. I was a bit bewildered by this. After all, if money could hear, that was news to me. We don't need to call forth inanimate objects. We simply need to seek God and make our requests known to him. When God comes on the scene, prosperity comes with Him. Healing comes. Joy comes. You name it. It comes as part and parcel of who He is. Not only does He have the whole world in His hands, He has everything we need in His hands.

> You have made known to me the path of life;
> you will fill me with joy in your *presence,*
> with eternal pleasures at your right hand.
> (Psalm 16:11)

Surely you have granted him eternal blessings
and made him glad with the joy of your *presence.*
(Psalm 21:6)

If you say you want the blessings of God, then what you really want is the presence of God in your life. In His presence all perfect gifts are found. I think of Esther, who had a life-and-death problem on her hands. So she fasted and prayed for three days. Then she put on her royal robes and went into the inner court to see her husband the king. Well, when he saw her he was pleased with her, extended his royal scepter to her, and asked her what she wanted. He would give her up to half of his kingdom if she wanted it. Whew! Don't you want a dress like the one she was wearing? It must have been something else to get a reaction like that. However, if I were to spiritualize this little scenario, I would have to say that our King is pleased to see us when we come into His inner court wearing robes of righteousness, an attitude of humility, a willingness to serve, and a worshipful spirit.

Esther then served the king a fine banquet and made sure that his every need had been satisfied. In return, the king asked what he could do for her. Still she held back her request, simply inviting him to come to dinner again! After the second meal the king was feeling so good he again asked her what could he give her. She had brought so much pleasure to his senses that he wanted to reciprocate. When we have made the heart of God full with our worship, our service, and our submission to His Lordship, He, too, asks, "What can I do for you? It is My pleasure to give you the kingdom!"

Have you placed the things that please God above your own desires? Do you curry His favor? What set Joseph, the son of Jacob, apart from his brothers? What did he do to earn that coat of many colors? The coat represented far more than the favoritism of his father; it signified authority.

49

Small wonder Joseph's brothers hated him. Yet Joseph sought the affection of his father by being the good son, so to speak. Joseph was the one his father relied on. Joseph honored his father. Jacob trusted Joseph with all that belonged to him. Why? Because Joseph drew close to Jacob's heart. He enjoyed being in the presence of his father. Jacob knew he had the undivided affections of his son. Can God say the same about you?

And what about King David? As I have mentioned before, he was no angel, yet God had a thing for David. He blessed David abundantly and secured an eternal legacy for his family. What was that all about? Well, think about it. Some call David the romantic warrior. He was always singing songs of worship to God. In his moments of extreme difficulty and fear, David chronicled his complaints, but he always ended by focusing on the abilities and mercies of God. David was a serious worshiper. And when he was wrong, he admitted it and was willing to accept the consequences.

After David angered God by taking a census, he realized the entire nation would suffer because of his decision. He asked God not to punish Israel for his sin. He made plans to buy a threshing floor so he could make a sacrifice to the Lord there and put an end to God's judgment. The owner of the floor offered to give it to David.

> But the king replied to Araunah, "No, I insist on paying you for it. I will not *sacrifice* to the LORD my God burnt offerings that *cost* me nothing." So David bought the threshing floor and the oxen and paid fifty shekels of silver for them. (2 Samuel 24:24)

> But King David replied to Araunah, "No, I insist on paying the full price. I will not take for the LORD what

is yours, or *sacrifice* a burnt offering that costs me nothing." (1 Chronicles 21:24)

David refused to be cheap with God. True worshipers know that they owe everything they have to God, and they hold back no part of their possessions or themselves. Remember, this is the same man who danced right out of his clothes in public, so unadulterated was his worship of the King of all creation. He who was king became a commoner in the sight of his heavenly King. Though David was king of Israel, he still humbled himself before the Lord of the universe gladly and with complete abandon. He held nothing back. His heart was an open door, giving God free reign to come and go as He pleased, to give and take whatever He desired. David was transparent in his worship. God knew He could trust David with any blessing because He knew David would gladly give it back. Because David withheld nothing, God knew He could give him everything.

God could say the same about Mary. He knew He could trust her to be the mother of His Son because He knew her whole heart belonged to Him. She drew near to God and sought Him in every circumstance. She was in constant communion with Him, open to His every word and instruction. She was a yielded vessel awaiting His visitation. Everything about her countenance, the way she carried herself, her walk and her talk said, *Yes, Lord.* Mary delighted God because He knew He had her attention. Her thoughts were oriented toward Him continually. From all that the scriptures indicate to me, I feel it is safe to conclude that Mary had surrendered to God all rights to her life. Therefore He knew that He could use her.

You see, true worshipers are unselfish. They will not superimpose their personal agenda over God's kingdom purposes. Their focus is solely on pleasing their Beloved. The only thing they long for more of is God Himself. Why? Because they've tapped into a secret.

> Thou wilt show me the path of life: In thy presence is *fullness* of *joy;* In thy right hand there are pleasures for evermore. (Psalm 16:11, ASV)

It doesn't get any better than that: fullness of joy, "pleasures evermore," as one translation says—I can go for all that, can't you?

Several friends I can think of bring me joy and pleasure. I want to be around them as much as possible because they brighten my day. When I'm not with them and I am in a situation I know they would enjoy, I think of them and make a mental note to repeat the activity with them. My thoughts are toward them because of the way I feel when I am with them. I reach out to them and do whatever I can to reciprocate the good times they have afforded me.

I believe that God is like that. When we bring Him joy and give Him pleasure, He thinks of all kinds of ways to reciprocate. When He knows that He is the center of our affection and that our hearts belong completely to Him, He knows that we will not be unfaithful lovers who squander His gifts. Then He freely gives without reservation. Yes, Mary could indeed magnify the Lord and sing of His faithfulness. He had answered her invitation to draw close to her. He had entered her personal space, searched her heart through and through, and found nothing wanting. They were intimate friends and confidantes. There were no secrets between Mary and her Lord. And so He chose to embrace her and deposit His Spirit within her to birth an extension of Himself—His only begotten Son. This was the most precious gift He could give her. The privilege of bearing what would be manifest to the world—His Word, living and breathing. Reflecting Him in the flesh. She would be the one who would feel His hand and His favor upon her. Not because of anything she did, but because of who she was.

A worshiper.

Thoughts to Ponder

- Are you a worshiper? What does your worship entail?
- Is your goal to put a smile on God's face every day? Are you filled with thoughts of pleasing Him?
- Are God's plans and desires foremost in your heart? Where does your personal agenda fit in with His design? What place in your heart does His kingdom purpose occupy?
- What in life is most important to you? Do you feel that you have completely surrendered your desires and goals to God?
- What does your worship cost you? Is God's blessing worth the sacrifice?

ears to hear

DISCERNING THE WORD OF THE LORD

> Mary was greatly troubled at his words and won-
> dered what kind of greeting this might be. But the
> angel said to her, "Do not be afraid, Mary, you have
> found favor with God."

LUKE 1:29-30

Can you imagine? There sat Mary talking—*with an angel!* When was the
last time *you* saw an angel? This has always blown my mind! It takes a
special pair of eyes to be able to see past flesh and blood into the realm of
the spirit. This experience is reserved for true worshipers who cross over
the portal of their fleshly limitations in order to press into the presence of
God. This is for the determined. Those who have made up their mind to
see God. These worshipers don't intellectualize God. They are open to the
moving of His Spirit yet are grounded in His Word. They press into His
presence until they get a word from Him. So great is their longing to hear
from heaven they forsake all other distractions and make the time to wait
on Him. These are the ones God meets. And when He comes, He speaks
profound truths that enable them to fulfill His kingdom purposes. He's no

heavenly psychic who's going to tell you what your man did last night. Such so-called "spiritualists" summon and get their information from "familiar" or demonic spirits. To venture into that arena can be dangerous. Remember, God is not a gossip or a soothsayer. When He speaks, He has a totally different conversation for our spirits to hear. His thoughts are higher than our thoughts and always Kingdom focused—even when giving us a personal word.

True worshipers are spiritually sensitive because they constantly practice the presence of God. They don't talk *at* God, they talk *to* Him. Then they stop, wait, and listen for an answer. They understand that prayer time is a time for *conversation* with God, not a one-sided monologue. The intimacy that is birthed during this time of regular exchange primes their spirit and the ears of their inner being to hear and know His voice. And when they are not in conversation with God, they are still mulling over, meditating, and rehearsing His words.

True worshipers recognize God's voice and that of His messengers. Think about it. You can easily recognize the voices of those you know well. Even if they try to disguise it you would be quick to say, "Oh, so-and-so, I know that's you!" Your close friends don't have to announce who they are when they call you on the phone because you have spent so much time together that you recognize the tiniest inflection of their voices.

HEAR WHAT THE SPIRIT SAYS

What about people who commit terrible crimes and swear God told them to do it? Obviously they got their wires crossed! So how *does* one know when the Spirit of God is speaking to them? Simple. God never goes against

His Word. He will never suggest or command something that doesn't line up with His written Word. Some might wonder about the instance when God told Abraham to sacrifice Isaac, but two important points apply to this case: First of all, God's Word was not yet documented. Second, God did not allow Abraham to complete the mission, thus being consistent with His Word even before it was written. He supplied a ram in the bush to be the sacrifice He had requested. God's command was simply a test for Abraham. Would he be willing to give to God what was dearest to Him? The answer was yes.

Since then, the Word has been preserved for our benefit so that on days when the noise of the world drowns out the voice of God or robs us of our ability to discern the leading of His Holy Spirit, we have a written mandate that renders us without excuse. This is why it is so important to know the Scriptures through and through, not in part but the whole.

> *Study* to shew thyself *approved* unto God, a workman
> that needeth not to be ashamed, rightly dividing the
> word of truth. (2 Timothy 2:15, KJV)

> The *sum* of Thy word is truth,
> And every one of Thy righteous ordinances
>   is everlasting. (Psalm 119:160, NASB)

Taking bits and pieces of God's Word out of the context of its entirety is dangerous. If you overhear a portion of a conversation, you are at risk of misunderstanding the overall content. This is why we must not dissect the Word of God without having a solid understanding of the whole. I always urge people to find a version of the Bible that is easy for them to comprehend, and then to read it all the way through like a novel before studying it topic by topic or book by book. This way you can see the big picture of God's heart and know that He is consistent in His views. Contrary to popular belief, the Bible does not contradict itself. God is not a schizophrenic God, one day feeling this way, the next day doing a total flip on us. No. He sticks to His guns. The disciple James said that God is so constant He doesn't change like shifting shadows (James 1:17). He is not moody. He remains true to Himself, to His Word. He is true to His Word because He *is* the Word. And that, my friend, is that!

But let's get back to recognizing God's voice. Knowing His mind and heart through His Word is crucial. What you know to be true about people makes a great difference in how you receive news or rumors about them. If someone delivered a message to you from your best friend and the content of that message was completely against his or her nature, the first thing you would say is, "That doesn't sound like my friend. I don't believe my friend said that! Let me double-check. You couldn't possibly have gotten that right." You would not receive a bad rumor about your friend because you know your friend's usual behavior. You have walked and talked with that person enough to know what he or she is likely to do or not do. If someone asked you how your friend would feel about a certain matter, you would know or could at least make a close guess.

We must know God's character just as well as we know our friend's character. If someone said God told her something that goes against His Word, you shouldn't have to think about it. By instinct you should reply, "That doesn't sound like God to me. He wouldn't say that."

We grow acquainted with God when we spend time in prayer conversing with Him, and He with us. We know when He is on the scene. We learn how He communicates with us: through His Word, by His Spirit, through dreams and visions, or by the confirming words of others who walk in the Spirit and give sound counsel.

> And it shall come to pass afterward, *that* I will pour out
> my spirit upon all flesh; and your sons and your daugh-
> ters shall prophesy, your old men shall dream *dreams,*
> your young men shall see visions. (Joel 2:28, KJV)

Sometimes, after you've shared your heart with the Lord and are waiting quietly in His presence for His response, He will impress a portion of Scripture on your mind for you to read that will be a word of instruction or comfort to you. Or by His Spirit He will communicate to your spirit and you will have a sense of deep knowing, a conclusion, and a peace about the subject you have laid before Him. Sometimes He sends someone to you who has the answer you seek. And sometimes He will speak to you in dreams and grant an interpretation, as he did with Joseph in the book of Genesis and Daniel in the book of Daniel.

What made Joseph so sure he had a word from God when he dreamed his dream? What made Joseph and Daniel so precise in their interpretations of other men's dreams? First, there was no mystery to the meaning of the dreams that God sent. I believe we have bad dreams, "pizza dreams," good dreams, and God dreams. Some dreams leave us shaken, worried, or exhausted. These are not from God. Even when He sends dreams to warn us, we have a sense of knowing that God has a solution already planned. He just wants you to be alert and aware of what is going on. When God deals with unbelievers or the disobedient, their dreams may be filled with news of coming judgment, as in the case of King Nebuchadnezzar and the baker in prison with Joseph. Sometimes the things foretold could be averted, sometimes not. So much for bad dreams. Good dreams just make us feel, well, good! They titillate our personal desires. But God dreams make an impact. They leave an impression on our spirits. We awake with a deeper understanding, a sense of purpose, or greater awareness of things to come.

> And he said, Hear now my words: If there be a prophet among you, *I* the LORD will make myself known unto him in a vision, *and* will speak unto him in a dream. (Numbers 12:6, KJV)

> Now a thing was secretly brought to me, and mine ear received a little thereof. In thoughts from the visions of the night, when deep sleep falleth on men... (Job 4:12-13, KJV)

I heard a preacher once say that God uses dreams to speak to those whose attention He cannot get during the day. But Scripture teaches that nighttime is when God whispers secrets to us, things for us to ponder in our heart, as Mary did. But more on that later. Being in touch with God constantly, even as we go on our way throughout the day, keeps us in tune to His voice whether we are asleep or awake. We should constantly apply ourselves to this communion with Him.

NIGHT SESSIONS

When I was still quite young in the Lord, I went on a seven-day fast to seek His direction for my life. During this time I had a dream. I couldn't shake it when I woke up. I pondered it, I shared it with my spiritual mentor, but I could not come to an understanding of what it meant. Even so, I knew that it was a message from the Lord to me.

The following Sunday a visiting minister spoke at my church. My mind drifted over my dream until the words of the sermon snatched me out of my musings. The minister was recounting a story that matched exactly what I had dreamed! He was using the story to make a point. As he continued his lesson, an understanding of what God had been saying to me became strikingly clear. He was encouraging me to overcome fear, something I was really struggling with at the time. I sat there weeping, so awed by the thought that I was important enough to God that He would send someone to speak words into my life in order to set me free. And God wants to be able to speak to all of us in a unique way that will get our attention and bless us.

Unfortunately, even the most spiritually sensitive person can become dull in the spirit and miss the voice of the Lord if he or she has become bogged down in selfish desires and ambitions. Our own agenda quite often crowds out the voice of the Lord. Consider Balaam, who was called by Balak, king of Moab, to come and curse the children of Israel (Numbers 22). The Lord told him not to go. But then the same ambassadors returned and offered Balaam a hefty reward for carrying out their request. For some reason Balaam thought this should change God's mind! This irritated God. He released Balaam to go, but not without a severe warning along the way. As Balaam made his way to meet the king of Moab, God sent an angel with a flaming sword to block his path. By now Balaam's sights were so set on the money, he didn't see the angel. But his donkey did.

After three temper tantrums and much abuse to the animal, which was trying to avoid its undoing at the hands of the angel, Balaam heard his donkey point out what he had failed to see. (Personally, that's when I would have been out of there.) Balaam could hear a donkey speaking but couldn't see the angel—go figure! Now it's a shame when an animal with the reputation for being dumb has more sense than you do. But that is what selfish ambition will do. It will kill your discernment and make you shortsighted. In Balaam's case, because the lives of others were involved, God made sure Balaam got the message. The angel made it clear that Balaam would be in deep trouble if he insisted on proceeding against the Word of the Lord. Well, that ended that drama. Truly the fear of the Lord is the beginning of wisdom (Proverbs 9:10). Balaam showed up on the scene and blessed the Israelites instead. His rationale to the king of Moab? "How can I curse what God has blessed?" The end. By God.

Now I haven't heard of any donkeys talking lately, so what does it take for you to get God's message? He has promised to give us instruction whenever we desire it.

> If any of you lacks *wisdom,* he should *ask* God, who gives generously to all without finding fault, and it will be given to him. (James 1:5)

> Whether you turn to the right or to the left, your ears will hear a voice behind you, saying, "*This* is the *way; walk* in it." (Isaiah 30:21)

> I will *instruct* you and teach you in the *way* you
>   should go;
> I will counsel you and watch over you. (Psalm 32:8)

What incredible promises! God will not only give us instruction, He will give us advice! This type of exchange is birthed out of having a relationship with One who cares for you deeply. I think of Jesus on the Mount of Transfiguration, when God sent Moses and Elijah down to talk with Him. Don't you want to know what they talked about? I suspect they were talking about the intricacies of dealing with God's people. It was a time of encouragement and refreshment for Jesus. Peter, James, and John were there. They had climbed up the mountain with Jesus. Notice that not *all* of the disciples went. Only these three: John, who longed to know the heartbeat of Christ so deeply that he laid his head against Jesus' breast; Peter, who received the revelation of who Jesus truly was and built His church on the foundation of that understanding; and James, who was the first of the twelve disciples to die for his faith. These were the three who held key positions in the birthing of the early church.

DOING WHAT IT TAKES

Peter, James, and John, though they did not understand the big picture of Jesus' ministry in the beginning, were not content merely to follow Christ and see if He would help them achieve their personal agendas—personal miracles, freedom from the Romans, financial security, whatever. No, they wanted more. They were men on a mission. They were in search of the kingdom of God. If Jesus knew the way to get to God, they wanted to go there. They were willing to follow Him as far as necessary to reach their heavenly goal. True worshipers go the extra mile to see the Lord as He truly is, and their efforts are rewarded.

> After six days Jesus took with him Peter, James and John the brother of James, and led them up a high mountain by themselves. There he was transfigured before them. His face shone like the sun, and his clothes became as white as the light. Just then there appeared before them Moses and Elijah, talking with Jesus.
>
> Peter said to Jesus, "Lord, it is good for us to be here. If you wish, I will put up three shelters—one for you, one for Moses and one for Elijah."
>
> While he was still speaking, a bright cloud enveloped them, and a voice from the cloud said, "This is my Son, whom I love; with him I am well pleased. Listen to him!" (Matthew 17:1-5)

Are you willing to come apart from the rest? To climb to another level? We tend to like mountaintop experiences only when they don't require anything of us. We like to build memorials to good feelings, but generally we are not allowed to remain there. We go up to get instructions and are then sent back down to live out what we have received. In every case where people in the Bible met God on a mountain—Moses, Elijah, Jesus—they were instructed to go back down and use what they had received from Him. In this life, those who go down willingly always find their way up again. God either leaves markers for them to find their way or supernaturally lifts them there with His own hands.

Such mountaintop experiences are available for all who truly want to hear God, and there is a difference between listening and hearing. Everyone knows a bad listener. Bad listeners insult us with their inattention. Yet they will insist that they are listening. When questioned on whether they truly heard us, they cannot repeat what we have just said. But God has a way of determining whether we have truly heard what He has said.

> Anyone who listens to the word but does not do what it says is like a man who looks at his face in a mirror and, after looking at himself, goes away and immediately forgets what he looks like. But the man who looks intently into the perfect law that gives freedom, and continues to do this, not forgetting what he has heard, but doing it—he will be blessed in what he does. (James 1:23-25)

Remember the mountaintop experience of the disciples? They were ready to just stay there and grow comfortable hanging out with Moses and Elijah, but God had a different plan. I called you all the way up here so you could hear my instruction, He said, and here it is: Listen to My Son and do what He says. Get refreshed by what Moses and Elijah share. Bask here for a minute but do not build a monument to the experience. There is work to be done, and I need you to hear Me and obey. Then you will be blessed.

HEARING AIDS

Spiritual hearing problems have a lot to do with our proximity to God. The further away we are from the Lord, the harder it is to hear Him. The pursuit of worldly knowledge rather than godly wisdom also gets many of us in trouble. The knowledge of good and evil or worldly philosophies alone robs us of the blessed life God wants to give us. It robbed Eve and it robs us. It is called living a lie. We are no smarter for our acquisition of knowledge because we still lack understanding, and wisdom demands that knowledge and understanding both be present in order to meet God's requirements of us. Yet God promises to be generous toward us when handing out wisdom. Knowledge plus understanding is what He requires of Himself, and the servant is not greater than the master.

> By wisdom the LORD laid the earth's foundations,
>> by understanding he set the heavens in place;
> by his knowledge the deeps were divided,
>> and the clouds let drop the dew. (Proverbs 3:19-20)

> Blessed is the man who finds wisdom,
>> the man who gains understanding. (Proverbs 3:13)

The tricky part is that we have so much besides wisdom to choose from. So many other trees—worldly philosophies of self-help, even some self-centered faith teachings—hold fruit that looks delectable. It is easy to remember our own spirits and forget God, to forget our source of blessing and mistakenly think that we are our own source. Nothing could be further from the truth.

> For although they knew God, they neither glorified him
> as God nor gave thanks to him, but their thinking
> became futile and their foolish hearts were darkened.
> Although they claimed to be wise, they became fools....
> They exchanged the truth of God for a lie, and

worshiped and served created things rather than the Creator—who is forever praised. Amen. (Romans 1:21-22,25)

Trust in the LORD with all your heart
    and lean not on your own understanding;
in all your ways acknowledge him,
    and he will make your paths straight.
Do not be wise in your own eyes;
    fear the LORD and shun evil.
This will bring health to your body
    and nourishment to your bones. (Proverbs 3:5-8)

Open your ears, hear "thus sayeth the Lord," and take heed. Mary did. She was not startled by His word to her; rather, she heard it and yielded to it. And she was blessed.

Thoughts to Ponder

- When was the last time you really heard from God?
- Do you readily recognize God's voice? How do you separate His instructions from your own longings?
- Do you welcome God's instruction even if it is contrary to your desires?
- In general, how do you respond to God's voice?
- How do you demonstrate that you have heard from God?

believing the unbelievable

DEVELOPING A WORKABLE FAITH

And *blessed is she* that believed: for there shall be a *performance* of those things which were told her from the Lord.

LUKE 1:45 (KJV)

I sat across from my two friends at a restaurant and smiled broadly. "So I hear you are getting married," I said to them. "Congratulations!"

My girlfriend looked quite surprised and exclaimed, "He told you that?!" She jabbed her boyfriend, my closest male friend, with her elbow. "I didn't believe him when he said it, so I didn't pay any attention to him. But since he has told you, I guess it's official!" I couldn't believe my ears. The girl didn't take her boyfriend seriously! It took my confirming his words for them to take root and kick her into action.

Later, as I mulled over the situation, I thought about the irony of it all. This woman had been waiting so long for the day when he would say he was ready to get married that when he finally and calmly made his announcement, she disregarded what he said. Her fear of disappointment had kept her from asking him whether he was truly serious. Therefore no plans had been made to finally secure her dream. Isn't that what we some-times do to God when He whispers a long-awaited promise in our ear?

Dare we hope He really means what He says? Perhaps if we don't grasp His words too tightly, we won't be disappointed. Yet He warns us that unbe-lief impairs our ability to receive from Him.

> In the same way, faith by itself, if it is not accompanied by action, is dead....
>
> You foolish man, do you want evidence that faith without deeds is useless? Was not our ancestor Abraham considered righteous for what he did when he offered his son Isaac on the altar? You see that his faith and his actions were working together, and his faith was made complete by what he did. And the scripture was ful-filled that says, "Abraham believed God, and it was credited to him as righteousness," and he was called God's friend. You see that a person is justified by what he does and not by faith alone....
>
> As the body without the spirit is dead, so faith with-out deeds is dead. (James 2:17,20-24,26)

How can you call someone a friend if you do not trust him? It actually hurts God's feelings when we don't believe what He says.

> And without *faith* it is *impossible* to *please* God, because anyone who comes to him must believe that he exists and that he rewards those who earnestly seek him. (Hebrews 11:6)

What does it take to please God? He simply wants us to trust and believe Him. Isn't that all we expect from our friends?

A friend of mine promised her daughter that she would make her a dress for a special occasion. The mother was so excited as she told me about the intricate design she was painstakingly working on to make the dress really special. Late in the night she would sit, sewing, anticipating the look of pleasure on her daughter's face when it would finally be finished. But because her daughter never saw her mother working on it, she kept questioning her mother about the dress. Was she really going to make it? When was she going to get started? Was she sure she would have it finished in time? On and on. My friend became so vexed at the lack of trust her daughter displayed that she finally exploded in frustration, "If you don't stop bugging me about that dress, I won't finish it!" She wanted to surprise her daughter. Her daughter's lack of faith in her took the joy out of the experience, and she grudgingly finished the dress without the special touches she had previously planned.

LOOKING HEAVENWARD

I think of Aaron, Moses' brother, left at the foot of the mountain while Moses went up to get a word from God for the people. Aaron didn't have enough conviction about the faithfulness of God to withstand the Israelites' unbelief. So he let them talk him into making an idol for them to worship. Meanwhile, back at the ranch (or should I say up on the mountaintop), God is making all kinds of elaborate plans for Aaron's life. Making him the head of the priesthood, outlining every detail down to what Aaron would wear! Aaron wasn't thinking about God, but God was thinking about him.

How embarrassed do you think Aaron was when God's plans were brought to light in spite of Aaron's bad behavior? How disappointed do you think God was with Aaron's inability to trust Him for a blessing? How many times do you think you've been in Aaron's shoes? Well, that's another thing to make you go "hmm."

Sometimes I think we kill the joy of blessing for God. Two things happen: We grieve His spirit by constantly questioning His motives, or we become paralyzed by our unbelief. Either way, we fail to take the steps that are necessary if we are to take hold of what God has prepared for us. It's like receiving a check in the mail and failing to cash it because we aren't sure it is legitimate, and then going on our way complaining about not having any money. It's like not using a gift God has given us because we don't believe we can prosper by it. This is a biggie. Why don't we step out in the area of our giftings? Because our faith is misplaced. We have turned our faith toward ourselves rather than God. "I don't think I can do it," we say, and we are absolutely right. But *God* can. Through *you!* As my friend Sherri Rose Shepard says, "He is God; you are not." Now that ought to set you free.

Our faith must be turned heavenward at all times. The average person feels bound by the expectations of others. How often have you said to someone who was trying to talk you out of doing something you had promised to do, "But they're counting on me"? Well, God doesn't like to disappoint us either. Yet He constantly suffers disappointment over our lack of trust in Him. Mary delighted God's heart. He told her something that sounded absolutely impossible, and she believed Him!

She told Joseph, her fiancé, what was about to happen. She didn't say, "Well, I'll wait until my body feels different and I know a baby is in there" before affirming what God had told her. She knew God's voice. She believed Him and acted on what He told her. After letting Joseph know, she went to visit her cousin Elizabeth, where she received further confirmation of what had been told her by God. You see, I believe the purpose of faith is two-fold. It warms God's heart that we believe Him, but it also propels us into action. Faith takes the check to the bank and cashes it. A check is no good until it is cashed. You can walk around broke with a million-dollar check in your pocket. Your poverty ends when you believe the bank has the resources to fill the order written on the check and you take the steps that are necessary to receive those resources. What makes us leave our money in banks? What makes us so sure it will be there when we need it? The same thing that makes us get on a plane and take for granted that we will reach our destination and disembark safely. One little word: faith.

> Now *faith* is being sure of what we hope for and certain
> of what we do not see. (Hebrews 11:1)

We put so much trust in technology and the ability of man without considering the likelihood that those things will disappoint us. How much more should we put our trust in God, who is truly able and faithful to do what He says? How can we be sure of what we hope for? How can we be certain of what we do not see? Because of the source of the promise.

> *God* is not a man, that he should *lie,*
> > nor a son of man, that he should change his mind.
> Does he speak and then not act?
> > Does he promise and not fulfill? (Numbers 23:19)

What hinders our faith? Could it be our preconceived notions of how God should or will act in a situation? Could it be our personal timetable of when we think that He should come through? It amazes me how often we assume the way in which God will carry out His promise to us. We stand looking to the left, waiting to see Him come over the horizon. All the while He is coming from the right. But we cannot see him, so we decide He is not coming. At other times the clock on the mantel of our hearts chimes the hour, and in the deafening silence that follows we begin to undress and settle in for a night of weeping, concluding we've been stood up. Then He appears in the morning, bringing His joy with Him. When questioned as to why He didn't come the night before, He looks at us quizzically and answers, "You never asked me when I was coming, so I believed you would wait."

UP CLOSE AND PERSONAL

Mary asked questions. She asked the angel how this most wonderful miracle of bearing God's Son was going to occur. Gabriel told her that the Holy Spirit would come upon her. The Son of God, the child she was to bear, would be conceived out of her intimacy with God Himself.

This is a "selah" moment—a time for us to stop and ponder. Everywhere in Scripture that a godly union led to conception the same words are used:

> And Adam *knew* Eve his wife; and she conceived. (Genesis 4:1, KJV)

> And Cain *knew* his wife; and she conceived. (Genesis 4:17, KJV)

> And Adam *knew* his wife again; and she bare a son. (Genesis 4:25, KJV)

> Elkanah *knew* Hannah his wife; and the LORD remembered her. (1 Samuel 1:19, KJV)

See the pattern? According to good old King James, the consummation of a godly union is always referred to as "knowing" the person. However, when the union was out of order—without love or covenant between the two—the King James translation makes a significant distinction, referring to the union with phrases such as "lay with" or "went in unto."

> And he [Abraham] *went in unto* Hagar, and she conceived. (Genesis 16:4, KJV)

> And when Shechem the son of Hamor the Hivite, prince of the country, saw her, he took her, and *lay with* her, and defiled her. (Genesis 34:2, KJV)

> And it came to pass, when Israel dwelt in that land, that Reuben went and *lay with* Bilhah his father's concubine. (Genesis 35:22, KJV)

> If a man be found *lying with* a woman married to an husband, then they shall both of them die. (Deuteronomy 22:22, KJV)

Isn't it interesting that intimacy without relationship is described as two people merely lying with one another? They are in fact perpetrating a lie which the world calls "making love." What Hagar, Sarah's maidservant, conceived when Abraham lay with her has caused troubles and war up to the present day because that union was nothing more than man's effort to produce God's promise. And man's efforts outside of covenant relationship with God, independent of God's guidance and blessing, will never produce any good thing. Lying together does not promote "knowing" one another, contrary to popular belief. The deception of the enemy is so subtle. Intimacy without covenant is a lie. God does not lie to us; He calls us to come into the full knowledge of who He is so that we can trust Him and conceive good things.

Now please! Do not go off on a tangent and run around saying that I said God had sex with Mary. *That is not what I am saying.* I am addressing the principle of intimacy. All of us who believe that the Bible is the written Word of God believe in the virgin conception. We believe Mary was overshadowed by the power of the Holy Spirit in the same way that Adam became a living soul by the breath of God. Mary conceived Jesus by that same breath, which brings life to the soul of every man and woman who drinks it in and allows him or her to be filled to overflowing with the very life of God.

GETTING IN SYNC

The mystery of becoming one with another person lies in the degree of intimacy you are willing to explore with that person. The more you know of him and the more time you spend with him, the more that person begins to rub off on you. You begin to absorb parts of his nature, and vice versa. I have a very special friend. When the two of us get together, people say it's like seeing and hearing everything in stereo. We have a lot of the same inflections. When we catch ourselves bursting into laughter at the same time or crossing our legs at the same time, we can't help but giggle because we are so delighted to be one in our sisterhood. Oh, to have that type of relationship with God! To be so in sync with His Spirit that we speak in stereo with His voice! That's what Jesus did.

> Jesus gave them this answer: "I tell you the truth, the
> Son can do nothing by himself; he can do only what he
> sees his *Father* doing, because whatever the *Father* does
> the Son also does." (John 5:19)

> Don't you believe that I am in the *Father*, and that the
> *Father* is in me? The words I *say* to you are not just my
> own. Rather, it is the *Father*, living in me, who is doing
> his work. (John 14:10)

When this type of closeness exists between friends, it is easy to trust each other implicitly. You know your friend has your heart, and vice versa. There is a knowing between the two of you. You sense the timing of the other person and rest in following that rhythm without question.

When I was working in advertising, the significant man in my life was a film director whom I hired quite often to shoot commercials for me. I always had a sense of peace when I worked with him because I knew we had the same vision. We liked the same things. We were connected. I would stand at one end of the set watching a scene and think to myself, "Hmm, they need to release the pigeons before he walks by." Before I could complete the thought in my head, I would hear him say, "They need to release the pigeons before he walks by." It would happen this way time and time again. The more I worked with him, the more I released projects to him and stayed out of the way. I trusted him to bring to life what was in my head. We had open communication. We shared and exchanged thoughts, ideas, our hearts, our dreams. We understood each other. I had faith in him. Therefore I could let go and allow him to do his thing and trust it to be right.

Knowing God in that way is crucial to having faith in God. When we know His character and His heart, we can believe even the seemingly ridiculous. I always chuckle when people say, "Put God in remembrance of His Word." As if He forgot! No, it is *we* who need to put *ourselves* in remembrance of His Word. It is for *our* sakes that we are to meditate on His words all the day long. To write them on our hearts, our foreheads, and our forearms, even as the priests of old did. Then, when He doesn't appear as *we think* He ought, *when* we think He ought, we will not panic. We will draw upon the things we know about Him and stand firm until He comes, doing what He said He would surely do. Sometimes when we think we are waiting too long, He is trying to get us more truly in sync with His heart. As we go through changes while waiting on God, I believe that He waits too. He waits for us to come up to a higher level of trusting Him. It's safe to say that none of us trusts Him as much as we should, no matter how great a level of faith we profess to possess. One trial is usually enough to prove it.

WHEN GOD STAYS AWAY

Mary and Martha sent a message to Jesus that their brother Lazarus was ill. The Scriptures say that Jesus stayed away *on purpose*. He actually waited for Lazarus to die! Then He announced to His disciples that Lazarus was asleep and that He wanted to go wake him up. The disciples thought this meant that Lazarus was taking a nap and recuperating, but Jesus went on to explain to them that, in earthly terms, Lazarus was dead. Lazarus was dead and Jesus was glad! Why? Because now He would have an opportunity to glorify His heavenly Father and prove that He had been sent by God.

Can you imagine the looks the disciples exchanged on that one? I love that about God. He refers to death as sleep—a temporary thing that does not interrupt life. We on earth see death as a permanent thing. The end. But God views it as a rest between breaths. A comma between earth and heaven! How much less we would grieve over the departure of loved ones if we could fully grasp this concept.

As Jesus approached the place where Lazarus lived, his sister Martha came out to greet Jesus and said, "If you had been here, Lazarus would not have died." Martha and Mary's unbelief made Jesus weep. His tears are often interpreted as grief over Lazarus's death, but Jesus had expressly stated that Lazarus was only sleeping. Jesus' statement reveals that the source of His tears was their unbelief. He had been with them so many times and shared so much, and still they did not understand all that He had taught them. They still couldn't conceive of what the Father was capable of doing through Him on their behalf. How much more does our lack of faith hurt the heart of God? Yet isn't that what we say to Him? "Where were you? If you had been here, this mess would not have occurred!" And then I think of Joseph going off to Egypt, sold into slavery, and the Bible says, "But the Lord was with Joseph." Then again, as he is thrown into prison, wrongly accused of rape, "But the Lord was with Joseph." If Joseph really was highly favored by God, how could these terrible things happen? Could it be that God knew He could trust Joseph to triumph in his trial and glorify Him? But when we're put through trials of our own, triumphing over them and glorifying God do not occur to us. I have a better understanding of why we miss opportunities like Joseph's when I consider what Jesus said to Martha next (in Michelle paraphrase): "I'm here now, and it's not over."

What Jesus really said was, "Your brother will rise again." Martha should have been able to accept that, coming from Jesus. After all, she herself had boldly proclaimed to Him that, even though it was late in the game, she knew God would give Him anything He requested. Yet when Jesus says, "Your brother will rise again," Martha is quick to reply that she knows he will rise in the resurrection at the *last day*. But that is *not* what Jesus said!

We can't get mad at Martha because we do the same thing. We put God in a box and put a lid on our faith because we don't know everything we need to know about Him. We, too, are quick to utter religious confessions and memorized scriptures by rote without examining their meaning. But Jesus is more patient than we are.

> Jesus said to her, "I am the resurrection and the life. He who believes in me will live, even though he dies; and whoever lives and believes in me will never die. Do you believe this?"
>
> "Yes, Lord," she told him, "I believe that you are the Christ, the Son of God, who was to come into the world." (John 11:25-27)

Again she misses the point. She doesn't make the connection between Jesus and the *present* situation. She puts His answer off into the future, a place where she won't have to exercise her faith in the moment. She has already determined everyone's fate based on her own finite understanding. Perhaps this is why we are not to lean to our own understanding, but rather to trust in God. Yet we put our faith in a cave and roll stones across the entrance, stifling the liberty that trusting God affords us.

> But some of them said, "Could not he who opened the eyes of the blind man have kept this man from dying?"
>
> Jesus, once more deeply moved, came to the tomb. It was a cave with a stone laid across the entrance. "Take away the stone," he said.
>
> "But, Lord," said Martha, the sister of the dead man, "by this time there is a bad odor, for he has been there four days."
>
> Then Jesus said, "Did I not tell you that if you believed, you would see the glory of God?" (John 11:37-40)

Ah, but perhaps this is where the disconnect occurs! Perhaps it is our *own* glory that we seek and not the *glory of God* in our everyday experiences. We would like to be comfortable, presenting a perfect image of perpetual victory to those around us and taking the credit. *Look at what a good little Christian I am. I am so tight with God that nothing touches me. I never have a problem. I possess the type of faith that can run though a troop and leap over a wall! Aren't I great?* All right, I'll start the confession—I've been guilty of this.

TAKING THE FAITH ROUTE

While I was struggling to recover from an injury I received when hit by a car (I was on foot), a friend said to me after my third surgery, "You haven't been healed because you don't have enough faith." I was furious. I retorted, "If it was just about faith, I would never have been hit in the first place. I never in my wildest dreams believed that God would allow something like this to happen to me!" And yet He did. Has this cost me my faith? No. I am following God's instructions and continuing to get better as I walk in obedience. Whenever I lag behind in the things He has told me to do, my injuries flare up. My faith and cooperation with God's instruction are a crucial part of the process of my physical healing. For some, He merely speaks the word and a quick work of healing is done. That's called a miracle. For others of us, the healing is a process because of what God wants to accomplish in our lives.

> Listen, my sons, to a *father's instruction;*
>> pay attention and gain understanding. (Proverbs 4:1)

> A wise son heeds his *father's instruction.* (Proverbs 13:1)

> Whoever gives *heed* to *instruction* prospers,
>> and blessed is he who trusts in the LORD.
>> (Proverbs 16:20)

Faith and obedience must walk hand in hand in order to reach the promise. Faith believes that the Father's instructions are right and willingly follows them, regardless of what our eyes see. Faith trusts the Father even when He leads us down a road that seemingly isn't taking us where we want to go.

Have you ever been given instructions to a place you've never been before? After driving for a while you begin to grow apprehensive if you don't see any markers along the way confirming that you're on the right track. You begin to doubt the instructions. You pull off to ask additional directions, or you call the person to make sure you are still heading down the right path. You find out that you are and are instructed to proceed. Your next question probably is "How far am I away from you? How much longer should it take me?" We feel more comfortable when we have a sense of the time frame surrounding our situation.

Well, sometimes God doesn't give us the time frame or the rationale for the route He has placed us on, and panic sets in. We worry. We fret. *Is He really going to do what He said?* We begin to poll our friends for reassurance. We turn off the path in search of a shortcut and become more turned around. Not so with Mary. She took God and His word without doubt. She asked how His promise would be accomplished and the answer came back, "By my Spirit." And that was enough for her. Her quiet trust supplied a fertile place for God to plant His promise. Her faith equipped her to birth the fruit of her expectations, and she was blessed.

Thoughts to Ponder

- Where do you really place your trust?
- Is your faith in God contingent upon what you see, hear, or feel?
- What evidence do you need to believe what God says to you?
- Are you following God's instructions?
- What is the level of your intimacy with God? Do you truly know Him, or are you embracing a lie?
- Are you in sync with God's Spirit? How do you know?

SIX

how does your garden grow?

DETERMINING YOUR HARVEST

And she cried out with a loud voice, and said, "Blessed among women are you, and blessed is the fruit of your womb!"

LUKE 1:42 (NASB)

It is said the fruit that grows closest to the vine is the sweetest. That makes sense to me. That which is closer to the source of nourishment is in a better position to receive the nutrients necessary for its enrichment. It would have first dibs on all the goodies, so to speak. The fruit further away would get the leftovers. I don't know about you, but I'm not fond of warmed-over goods. I like my food fresh, hot off the press. Kind of like information. The closer you are to the original story, the better chance you have of possessing the facts.

Likewise, when we get God's Word firsthand, the revelation is powerful, life-changing. One word from God is enough to renew your mind. Transform your life. Make you look different. Walk in a different way. Do

85

something you've never done before. If you see the words on the page as nothing more than arranged letters, that's not enough to revolutionize your world. But when you get in God's face and allow Him to breathe on the Word you've absorbed, it comes to life and bears fruit!

A seed looks like absolutely nothing until it's pressed into fertile soil and watered. It sits for a while looking the same, and then it dies. Just when you think it's over, something happens. The pressure of what is deep within it breaks open that ol' dry, dead shell. New life bursts forth. It begins to grow roots and grab hold of the earth around it to anchor itself. Once the seed has taken a firm grip, it extends itself upward and reveals what has been inside of it all along—scrumptious fruit for others to behold, partake of, and enjoy. Are you aware of the joy that can be found in feeding others with what God has planted inside of you? Truly, producing fruit is the greatest part of the blessed life.

> The Lord Jesus himself said: "It is more *blessed* to *give*
> than to receive." (Acts 20:35)

I love to give things away, anything from a word of encouragement to a gift I know someone will enjoy. I love seeing the look that crosses recipients' faces as they receive. I am fed as I feed others. When I withhold from others, I rob myself of joy. Because being fruitful is an important part of the call God has placed on the lives of all who know Him, it stands to reason that after the Fall in the Garden of Eden, the desire to be fruitful became the focal point of human effort. In their quest for knowledge, Adam and Eve became self-centered instead of God-centered. They had the knowledge but not the ability to produce what God had produced so easily: Eve would bear children in difficulty, and Adam would sweat to reap what had once literally fallen into his hands before. Their relationship would also suffer as selfish ambition drove them to try to control each other. The man and the woman were not cursed; their ability to be fruitful apart from God was cursed.

HANG IN THERE

But Jesus would come onto the scene through the womb of Mary. God would once again be the originator of the fruit, and the curse would be broken as His Son was broken for us! The fruit of Mary's womb was blessed, and now His life within us will produce fruit as long as we cling to Him in an intimate embrace.

> Remain in me, and I will remain in you. No branch can *bear fruit* by itself; it must remain in the vine. Neither can you *bear fruit* unless you remain in me.
> I am the *vine;* you are the *branches.* If a man remains in me and I in him, he will bear much fruit; apart from me you can do nothing. (John 15:4-5)

Here is where our war with new age religion begins. New age religion teaches that *you* are your *own* source, that *you* are the one who makes things happen, that *you* control your destiny. There is some truth in this way of thinking in that you choose whether or not to cooperate with God. Because God has given us free will, our decisions do indeed set our course. But new-age philosophy suggests that you are entirely the captain of your own ship. You are a little god. Your *own* god. Nothing could be further from the truth.

There is only one God, and He will not share His glory with another. Yet He will allow you to build your own personal kingdom and then watch it topple because no foundation except the Solid Rock is stable.

When we stand on God's promises, abide in Him, and allow Him to be the source of our life's fruit, whether attitudinal or material, we thrive. We prosper. It's all good! *Good fruit.* God is delighted with good fruit. Why? Because it fosters spiritual germination and health in all who partake of it. Producing life in others. Multiplying. Producing more fruit after its own kind—meaning more believers living completely sold-out lives for God. We should be adding to the kingdom, as God's good fruit in us attracts others who seek nourishment. What was God's first command to Adam? "Be fruitful and multiply." This command is issued to every believer.

> You did not choose me, but I chose you and appointed you to go and *bear fruit—fruit* that will last. Then the Father will give you whatever you ask in my name. (John 15:16)

> So, my brothers, you also died to the law through the body of Christ, that you might belong to another, to him who was raised from the dead, in order that we might *bear fruit* to God. (Romans 7:4)

> And we pray this in order that you may live a life worthy of the Lord and may please him in every way: *bearing fruit* in every good work, growing in the knowledge of God. (Colossians 1:10)

We were chosen to bear fruit. God planted His Spirit within us that we might produce good works that glorify Him. He wants us to bear fruit that makes the sacrifice of Jesus worthwhile.

Have you ever put in a good word for someone, gone the extra mile to pave the way for an opportunity for them? When they do a good job and the person to whom you recommended them comes back to thank you for the reference, you feel as if your efforts were worth your while. On the other hand, if the person turns out to be a disappointment or a disgrace to you, it is easy to wonder why you ever bothered. Do you think Jesus looks at you and says it was worth all the trouble He went through to die for you? Is your life producing things that make Him glad He endured the shame of the cross because of the joy you now bring to Him through the fruit of your life? Or are you experiencing spurts of growth, mere samplings of what could be, but no fruit that lasts?

PASSING FRUIT INSPECTION

What type of fruit lasts? The fruit of the Spirit at work in your personal life and in the souls of others—souls drawn to the kingdom because of what your life testifies about God. Souls called into His marvelous light will live eternally in His presence. His life in you is supposed to produce more life. More fruit. And lush fruit draws God's indulgence. Jesus said that when you are fruitful the Father will give you whatever you request. How can He guarantee such a thing? Because He knows that when you are truly bearing fruit you won't ask for anything that won't produce more fruit. You will be so tapped into the vine that you will know instinctively what is not conducive to your continued growth, and you won't even go there. You will be sold out to your sole purpose—glorifying God.

> This is to my Father's glory, that you *bear* much *fruit,*
> showing yourselves to be my disciples. (John 15:8)

We make God look good when we bear fruit. We affirm where we truly stand and to whom we belong. Why should God bless people who make Him look bad? I have never witnessed a parent reward a child for embarrassing him or her in public. Unfruitful Christians are a disappointment to God and an embarrassment to His kingdom. Unfruitful in attitude. Unfruitful in deeds. Both should cause us to hang our heads in shame.

Think of how you have felt during the publicized fall of any great man or woman of God. Their bad fruit leaves a lot of explaining for you to do to those around you who are not Christians. It sets the Christian community back for a minute. We all struggle collectively to recover, hoping the memory of this disgrace will quickly fade so we can get back to witnessing effectively. We are deeply grieved over this poor advertisement for the kingdom, and we realize that now our job has become more difficult. Yet we can't draw back, for to do so would be to stifle the part of our very nature that lives to share Christ's life with others. When you abide in the vine, such sharing comes as naturally as breathing. It is an act of worship to God to reproduce what He has given you. This is your reason for being. Your very purpose, the fulfillment of which brings a smile to God's face and great blessings to your life.

It is important to note that unfruitful Christians are not victorious Christians because they do not attract the blessings of God. Some may say, "Well, isn't fruit itself a blessing?" My answer is that the fruit of *your* fruit—

the byproduct of your original fruit—is the blessing. Stay with me here. You are told to be fruitful and multiply. So multiply your fruit. Your first fruit goes to God in response to His command, which is to produce the fruit of the Spirit that draws others to Him:

> Now he who supplies seed to the sower and bread for food will also supply and increase your store of seed and will enlarge the harvest of your righteousness. You will be made rich in every way so that you can be generous on every occasion, and through us your generosity will result in thanksgiving to God.
>
> This service that you perform is not only supplying the needs of God's people but is also overflowing in many expressions of thanks to God. Because of the service by which you have proved yourselves, men will praise God for the obedience that accompanies your confession of the gospel of Christ, and for your generosity in sharing with them and with everyone else. (2 Corinthians 9:10-13)

Your obedience sets a multiplication factor in motion: Your fruit produces and multiplies more fruit for the kingdom. God then blesses your obedience, which causes you to experience an overflow. The overflow is what blesses *you*. The overflow is the extra-dimensional blessing of God, which you receive because the fruit of the Spirit is evident in your life first. This pleases God and promotes you with man. Are you getting this? Lush fruit gets God's attention and blessings, but He turns His face away from what does not please Him.

Unfruitfulness is not a pretty picture in God's eyes. Small wonder Jesus was so upset with that old tired fig tree. It was defying its reason for existing by being unfruitful.

> Early in the morning, as he was on his way back to the city, he was hungry. Seeing a fig tree by the road, he went up to it but found nothing on it except leaves. Then he said to it, "May you never bear fruit again!" Immediately the tree withered. (Matthew 21:18-19)

Whoa! Now that's deep. Some Christians are like that—all foliage and no fruit. God isn't interested in the fancy garnish for show; He wants to sample and partake of the fruit of our lives. When He visits us and finds our fruit bitter or nonexistent, He removes our ability to produce more of the same. God cannot allow fruitlessness to abound. An overgrowth of fruitless branches will sap all the life out of the plant and out of the ground it is planted in. They leave no room or opportunity for the good fruit to spring forth. And that's a no-no. So in essence Jesus was saying (in Michelle paraphrase), "Look, if you're just going to stand around being unproductive, there is no reason for you to be here."

> Then he told this parable: "A man had a fig tree, planted in his vineyard, and he went to look for fruit on it, but did not find any. So he said to the man who took care of the vineyard, 'For three years now I've been coming to look for fruit on this fig tree and haven't found any. Cut it down! Why should it use up the soil?'

"'Sir,' the man replied, 'leave it alone for one more year, and I'll dig around it and fertilize it. If it bears fruit next year, fine! If not, then cut it down.'" (Luke 13:6-9)

God will do whatever He can to help jumpstart the bearing of fruit in our lives. If we don't respond, however, we will find ourselves cut off from opportunities that were once available to us in order to make room for those who will be more productive. This brings us back to operating according to our purpose. Our purpose is to be fruitful by utilizing our gifts and talents to bless people around us, and then to allow that fruit to be the catalyst that draws them to God and multiplies the kingdom.

In the same way, let your light shine before men, that they may see your *good* deeds and praise your Father in heaven. (Matthew 5:16)

Live such *good* lives among the pagans that, though they accuse you of doing wrong, they may see your *good* deeds and *glorify* God on the day he visits us. (1 Peter 2:12)

The servant who knows his master's will and does not get ready or does not do what his master wants will be beaten with many blows. But the one who does not know and does things deserving punishment will be beaten with few blows. From everyone who has been

given much, much will be demanded; and from the one
who has been entrusted with *much, much* more will be
asked. (Luke 12:47,48)

For everyone who has will be given more, and he will
have an abundance. Whoever does not have, even what
he has will be taken from him. (Matthew 25:29)

In the last scripture above, so goes the story of the unproductive servant
who was given a talent and did not use it (Matthew 25:14-30). The good
master had distributed talents among his workers according to what he knew
to be their ability. Two of the servants invested theirs wisely and used them
to gain a greater return for the master. But the third servant buried his and
gave the original talent, a little crusty and mildewed from being hidden,
back to the master. This did not bring accolades from his superior. Rather,
the master took the unused talent from the unproductive servant and gave
it to the one he knew would use it. Likewise, God is a wise investor.

PROVING YOUR WORTH

No matter our station in life, we must use what we have at our disposal.
Saints cannot afford to sit around looking for a handout. That is not how we
get blessed or gain favor. We must put to work the talents that God has placed
within us. Invest your gifts wisely by blessing others with them—then watch
the doors fly open, ushering you into the presence of great blessings.

But what is your gift? I will say this in every book I write if I have to:
Your gift is the thing you do well because it is second nature to you. Others

notice and celebrate what you do, even though it may seem like nothing to you. That's your gift. Some have the gift of cooking, cleaning, hospitality, organization, decoration, working with children—you name it—not everyone does it well. In Proverbs 18:16 (NASB), we are told that our gifts make room for us. In other words, your gift, when set before those who need what you have to offer, opens the door to favors and blessings. No job should be viewed as despicable or undesirable. Every job, whether seemingly menial or noteworthy, fills a need. Can you imagine what the world would be like if no one cleaned the rest rooms in public facilities? They would be filthy, and disease would run rampant! Some people are good at cleaning and have prospered from doing it by establishing cleaning companies or doing it themselves for clients. What is your gift? What are you good at? Be fruitful and use it for God's glory.

GOING WITH THE FLOW

Let's take a look at the life of Joseph. He went from being the favorite in his father's house, pampered on every side, to being a slave in a foreigner's house. You don't think he rose to the position of overseeing Potiphar's house in a day, do you? Absolutely not! Israelites were like dogs in the eyes of the Egyptians, who fancied themselves far more sophisticated and advanced than any other society in the earth. No, Joseph started with the most menial of tasks. He applied himself to these drudgeries, performing them with a spirit of excellence, to the glory of God, and God honored him by causing everything he touched to prosper. So of course Joseph got promoted.

You may know the rest of the story. Potiphar's wife took a liking to him, and when he refused to respond to her advances, she accused him of rape and had him thrown into jail. But even there he decided to be the best convict that he could be. Again God honored him, and Joseph was promoted. I love how Jacob, Joseph's father, described Joseph's response to these difficult situations:

> Joseph is a fruitful vine,
>   a fruitful vine near a spring,
>   whose branches climb over a wall.…
> because of your father's God, who helps you,
>   because of the Almighty, who blesses you
> with blessings of the heavens above,
>   blessings of the deep that lies below,
>   blessings of the breast and womb.
> Your father's blessings are greater
>   than the blessings of the ancient mountains,
>   than the bounty of the age-old hills.
> Let all these rest on the head of Joseph,
>   on the brow of the prince among his brothers.
>   (Genesis 49:22,25-26)

I just love that passage! Jacob praises the fact that Joseph drew his strength from the Spirit of God and survived—no, *overcame*—his circumstances. He was anchored in his relationship to God, the true vine, drawing from His living waters to sustain himself in tough times and situations. Joseph set his sights on maintaining a godly attitude and being an excellent servant, though surely he must have chafed under his seeming reversal of fortune. He decided to learn the necessary lessons and come out the victor.

He put his hand to the grindstone and used what he had—his ability to serve—where he was. He flourished in the midst of his trial and, by God's grace, made something out of the lot that had been given him. And because of Joseph's obedient and willing attitude, God blessed him. He himself proclaimed, "God has made me fruitful in the land of my affliction."

Fruitful people allow themselves to be purged of all that is not needed to produce what God has called them to. Fruitful people are overcomers no matter what! They can take a licking and keep on ticking, as the old Timex advertisement said. Why? Because fruitful people continue to cling to the vine and draw strength from it. They know their ultimate assignment is to glorify God. And they know who alone can help them accomplish that end.

> Surely God is my *help;*
>> the *Lord* is the one who sustains me. (Psalm 54:4)

> My help comes from the LORD,
>> the Maker of heaven and earth. (Psalm 121:2)

But let's talk once more about that fruit. What kind of fruit does God like? What type of fruit does He smile upon and bless? Fruit that is borne from the seed God Himself plants within us through the deposit of His Holy Spirit. As His own Spirit works within us, as we yield to the lessons He teaches and cooperate with His instructions, we cultivate a crop that is pleasing to God. But if we resist His Spirit, we sow an entirely different crop in our field. Again, the choice is ours to choose kindness over insensitivity, goodness over cruelty, love over bitterness, gentleness over harshness.

God gives us the option between yielding to the works of the flesh or allowing the fruit of the Spirit to bloom within us. He equips us with everything we need to do what pleases Him, but He won't force us to produce. If we truly love Him, we will choose the fare He likes.

> But the fruit of the Spirit is love, joy, peace, patience, kindness, goodness, faithfulness, gentleness and self-control. (Galatians 5:22-23)

How I struggled with this verse when I first came to the Lord! I tried to behave like all the wonderful Christians around me, but I just could not be like them. Finally in the midst of my despairing to the Lord, He spoke to me and said, "Michelle, I didn't call you to be a cookie-cutter Christian. I don't want you to mimic others and try to be like everyone else. I want you to be you and to allow Me to be who I am in you. If you would allow Me to operate through you, using your unique personality, we could be quite a team." Well, that set me free. I allowed Him to adjust my habits (and even my wardrobe) instead of adjusting myself to the example of others. My life and character were transformed as I studied God's Word and renewed my mind with His perspective. I responded to His voice as He instructed me on what was good and what was unbecoming, and it was easy to obey because His instructions were so loving!

Once I let go of trying to toe the line in my own flesh, I found myself flowing in God's love, joy, peace and all of the above a whole lot more easily. I allowed His Spirit to rise up inside of me. I gave Him permission to overtake my flesh and cause me to be fruitful. Just like Mary. But every time I took the reins back into my own hands, I stumbled into error and felt the strain of dead works done in the flesh.

WORKING IT OUT

Because it's true that God lives in us and produces love, that the joy of the Lord is our strength, that He promises to give us the peace of God that surpasses all understanding by Christ Jesus, that patience does its own perfect work in us if we let it, then why do we grunt, groan, work, and stress? We are told to simply abide in Him. Relax, relate, release, and go with the flow of His Spirit. Leave the driving to Him, in a sense, and you will arrive at the destination of fruitfulness.

Pack up your stuff and get in the car, but don't grab the wheel! Don't be Sarah, Abraham's wife in the book of Genesis, who tried to make God's promises happen and added confusion to the plan. Stay sensitive to His leading and don't run ahead of the program. But don't lag behind either. Give God something to work with. That something would be *you*—yielded, available, and ready to be used. Allow *Him* to open doors of opportunity for blessing. It's your job to be equipped and prepared to embrace whatever He brings your way. When I wrote my first book, I had no idea where to begin to get it published. I just knew that it would one day be in print. As I wrote my manuscript, opportunities came my way, and I was ready to present something when asked what I had to offer. I did my part; God did His. The end. By the Holy Ghost.

Mary didn't have to do anything to conceive the seed that bore God's firstfruit. She simply said yes to God. She didn't try to help God; she merely cooperated. There is a difference. She didn't go off in search of a partner to guarantee her pregnancy. No, she rested in what she was told and waited on God. She yielded to Him her flesh and the limitations of her understanding. He was able to work with a surrendered vessel. Because she presented to Him a heart that was pliable in His hands, He was able to plant what He wanted in her life. He blessed His living Word within her womb. She received it and allowed it to become a perfect work in her. And the fruit of her womb was blessed.

Thoughts to Ponder

- Have you taken stock of your fruit lately? What's it like? Do you bear more foliage or more fruit?
- Are you nurturing life in others around you? Are their lives different because of you?
- When do you try to be fruitful in the flesh versus allowing the Spirit to have control?
- What are your talents or gifts? Are you using them to bless others?
- What type of advertisement are you for the kingdom of God?

SEVEN

standing for something, falling for nothing

CHOOSING THE PATH OF GREATEST REWARD

But the angel said to her, "Do not be afraid, Mary, you have found favor with God. You will be with child and give birth to a son, and you are to give him the name Jesus. He will be great and will be called the Son of the Most High. The Lord God will give him the throne of his father David, and he will reign over the house of Jacob forever; his kingdom will never end."

LUKE 1:30-33

Looking back on heroes of old, one is struck by their determination to stand firm in the face of great opposition and misunderstanding. These were the ones who kept their heads when around them everyone else was losing theirs. They did not waffle at difficulty or lose heart in the face of adversity. They had a vision in mind, a great cause. Usually it involved the saving of a nation. Such heroes were willing to give their lives for what they believed in. People like William Wallace of Scotland, Joan of Arc of France, Gandhi, Martin Luther King Jr., and many others gladly gave their lives in an effort to redeem the lives of others. Some did not live to see what their efforts wrought, but their sacrifices were worth it because embedded in their hearts was belief in their mission. For them, abandoning the cause would have been worse than death.

Today, when political candidates run for office, debates rage over their stand on the issues. We are quick to criticize them if they seem to shift and change their opinions to please special-interest groups. Our disdain for them escalates if they seem indecisive about issues. We decide they cannot be trusted. No trust, no vote. No vote, no victory for that candidate. Why? Because we've been taught that the person who doesn't stand for something will fall for anything. I think that boils down to being double-minded. In the eyes of man or of God, double-mindedness is not a good quality.

> He who doubts is like a wave of the sea, blown and tossed by the wind. That man should not think he will receive anything from the Lord; he is a double-minded man, unstable in all he does. (James 1:6-8)

THE BLESSING BUSINESS

When it comes to the issue of blessings, God searches our hearts to see where we stand. Where do we stand in Him? Where do we stand on kingdom issues? His evaluation determines what He can trust us to possess.

Obviously Mary could be trusted with His Son. God knew, based on Mary's heart condition, that she would raise Jesus in the right fashion and groom Him for His life mission. She would not be selfish but would remember that He was God's Son first. Jesus was not born to give Mary emotional comfort or to validate her as a woman. He was born to redeem the souls of mankind. In order for her to be able to release Him to His mission, God had to be her all-consuming passion. God, not her son, had to be the One who filled her heart to overflowing. She had to be consumed with God's desire for the salvation of the world. She had to be in agreement with His plan. Yes, for this very special assignment God searched the hearts of countless women and found Mary's heart not wanting for anything. All of this is not to say that Mary was perfect by any stretch of the imagination. After all, she was human, but the bottom line was her heart condition. It is my belief, whatever her mistakes, that she kept short accounts with God and did not abuse His grace. When God looked at her heart He found a heart sold out to Him and so He took up residence there. In order to be blessed above measure, we must deal with our hearts and decide where we stand.

> Come near to God and he will come near to you. Wash your hands, you sinners, and purify your hearts, you *double-minded.* (James 4:8)

Why is being double-minded associated with impure hearts? Because the heart is the seat of the will, the place where we come to conclusions and make decisions. The heart influences our every move. Depending on whom or what we love most, we choose our course of action. We operate according to either a selfish strategy or a heavenly agenda.

Do not store up for yourselves treasures on earth, where moth and rust destroy, and where thieves break in and steal. But store up for yourselves treasures in heaven, where moth and rust do not destroy, and where thieves do not break in and steal. For where your treasure is, there your heart will be also....

No one can serve two masters. Either he will hate the one and love the other, or he will be devoted to the one and despise the other. You cannot serve both God and Money. (Matthew 6:19-21,24)

Those whose hearts are God-centered, who live with kingdom purpose at the forefront of their thoughts, are blessed and highly favored to eat from the fat of the land.

> The heart is deceitful above all things and beyond cure.
>   Who can understand it?
> "I the LORD search the heart
>   and examine the mind,
> to reward a man according to his conduct,
>   according to what his deeds deserve."
>   (Jeremiah 17:9-10)

Let's look at this heart thing in every context, from emotional to physical to material blessings. Consider Abraham, an extremely wealthy man. God could trust him with wealth because Abraham was sold out to God. He was not a hoarder. Can God trust you with money? Do you still go through a battle when it's time to give your tithes and offerings? Do you still quibble over whether to tithe your gross or your net? I'm just trying to make a point, not offend you. Abraham gladly gave to Melchizedek, the first high priest mentioned in Scripture, a tithe off all he had acquired after winning a tremendous battle. Even when dividing the land between Lot and himself so they could all live peaceably, Abraham did not insist on the best for himself. Instead, he allowed Lot to choose the better area. Abraham continued to trust that God would bring him into the fullness of His inheritance, and Lot's choices could not stop that from happening. In Abraham's mind, God was well able to guard His interests, keep His promises, and fulfill His kingdom agenda. After all, Abraham was merely being obedient to God's order to move out and possess the land. It was *God,* not Abraham, who wanted to establish a nation. Abraham was simply walking in cooperation with God. The bottom line was that Abraham had no agenda other than God's.

HEART'S DESIRES, HEAVEN'S INQUIRIES

Now look at Hannah, who so dearly wanted a child (1 Samuel 1). She also came to the place of releasing her selfish agenda. Perhaps she thought long and hard on a comment her husband, Elkanah, made. He had inquired of her, "Why are you downhearted? Don't I mean more to you than ten sons?" Elkanah gave her a double portion to offer to the Lord just because he loved her, not because of anything she did. In fact, by the worldly standards of the day she was a failure not worthy of a reward. Elkanah's other wife, Peninah, had borne him several children, but Hannah had not birthed one. Elkanah did not care about Hannah's performance; he only saw her heart and loved her. Likewise, I think God looks at our heart condition and loves us, bestowing double portions on those whose hearts long to produce fruit not for our own personal gain but for the kingdom.

Hannah focused on the reason for her desire and chose to make the only sacrifice that would truly be a sacrifice to her. She vowed to release her firstborn into the service of the Lord. She chose to give that which was dearest to her back to Him! Can you imagine waiting years for a son, only to finally get one and have to leave him at the temple? Yet that was exactly what Hannah did. She gave God her first fruit, and He in turn gave her a rich harvest, a crop of children in addition to the one she had given over to Him for the furtherance of His purposes.

Hannah had come to the place of realizing that having children was not about gaining personal satisfaction or even validation as a woman in the eyes of her husband and society. Her first call was to produce a child to the glory of God. She did that by releasing Samuel to be groomed as a mighty prophet for the Lord. And for this offering to the Lord, she gained the regard of God and was richly blessed above and beyond what she could have asked or imagined.

Just as Elkanah asked Hannah, God asks us the question, "Don't My love and My purposes mean more to you than the blessings you long for?" Whatever is on our wish list   be it riches, love, prominent position—we must be willing to render these things back to the Lord. Then and only then can He trust us with them. When He finds a heart that can truthfully say, "Yes, Lord, I'm willing to sacrifice everything for your sake," then He pours out such a wealth of blessings that we cannot contain them all. If we are double-minded about our commitment to God and the furtherance of His kingdom, our vats will dry up.

What about David? His mind was consumed with using his great wealth to build a temple for God. Yet God would not allow him to build it because he had been a man of war and had blood on his hands. The Lord allowed David to contribute goods for the building of the temple and continued to bless David with material goods to overflowing *because he knew where David's heart was.* David's heart was consumed with pleasing God, with lifting Him up for all to see. David's passion went beyond leading Israel; David's passion was to establish God's kingdom on earth. David wanted to give God His due—a place designated for worshiping Him— and in David's heart even that wouldn't have been enough. Although David was not able to carry out this desire, God honored David's heart toward Him. Even after David had acquired houses, lands, gold, and more, God was his first love.

FOR THE LOVE OF MONEY

Money and power truly reveal our hearts. Position, status, and wealth have been the downfall of many a great man and woman of God. With these things in hand, they have gotten off of their knees and onto their own course, forgetting all the wonderful plans they had to glorify God if only they had enough money or influence to do so.

Solomon was guilty of this. He started off so well. He had seen what God had done for his father, David. Now that the throne belonged to him, he purposed to carry on in the tradition of his father and be a worshiper first and a king second, totally relying on the guidance of the Lord.

> At Gibeon the LORD appeared to Solomon during the
> night in a dream, and God said, "Ask for whatever you
> want me to give you."

Solomon answered, "...give your servant a discerning heart to govern your people and to distinguish between right and wrong. For who is able to govern this great people of yours?"

The Lord was pleased that Solomon had asked for this. So God said to him, "Since you have asked for this and not for long life or wealth for yourself, nor have asked for the death of your enemies but for discernment in administering justice, I will do what you have asked. I will give you a wise and discerning heart, so that there will never have been anyone like you, nor will there ever be. Moreover, I will give you what you have not asked for—both riches and honor—so that in your lifetime you will have no equal among kings." (1 Kings 3:5-6,9-13)

But with the acquisition of these things, Solomon also acquired more opportunities to be distracted by ungodly women and all the material things his wealth could afford him. His heart turned away from the purposes of God toward his own designs, and he fell. He began to worship the gods of his foreign wives and offended God. On that note, he also fell out of favor with God. He ended his days sighing, "Vanity of vanities! All is vanity" (Ecclesiastes 1:2, NASB). If all we heap up for ourselves does not have God's favor and blessing, it becomes an empty acquisition that cannot be fully enjoyed.

The lust of the eyes, the lust of the flesh, and the pride of life are the original sins still at work in our lives today. The Holy Spirit is also at work, searching the hearts of all those who profess to love God: Who can be trusted among us with the blessings we ask for? And yet God desires to bless us and shower His favor on us. So determined is He to bless us that He is willing to break us first, as he did with Joseph.

Yes, God was going to promote Joseph, but only when Joseph was ready to handle the promotion. I heard a preacher once say that God is ready to bless you when you are ready to be blessed. Now that is deep. I'll repeat it again: God is ready when you are ready, when you finally have His heart toward the matters set before you. Joseph understood that his newfound position as the right-hand man to Pharaoh was not about him. It wasn't about saying, "Nah, nah, na, na, nah" to his brothers. It was about God placing him in a position where he was able to carry out God's agenda: saving the nation of Israel. Why do you want what you want? Why do you dream of what you dream of? Think about it.

Because it is God who blesses with wealth, let's think about why He would. So we can buy more shoes? (That's *my* weakness! The Lord knows I love a beautiful pair of shoes!) No! Absolutely not! As my mother would say whenever I left food on my plate, "There are children starving in Ethiopia and other portions of the world." So why would He bless us with wealth? Why would He put large sums of money into our hands? Because He wants us to distribute it to those in need.

> "Bring the whole tithe into the *storehouse, that there may be food in my house.* Test me in this," says the LORD Almighty, "and see if I will not throw open the floodgates of heaven and pour out so much blessing

that you will not have room enough for it." (Malachi 3:10)

God wants provision to be available to those who need to see His benevolence manifested in their lives. What a privilege it is when you can be a partner with Him in this! This is one of the ways we glorify God, and He blesses us in return. We cannot beat God in our giving. Neither can we deny that blessing His children is the desire of His heart. His Word on why He chooses to give or withhold is clear.

> When you ask, you do not receive, because you ask with wrong motives, that you may spend what you get on your pleasures. (James 4:3)

> Religion that God our Father accepts as pure and faultless is this: to look after *orphans* and *widows* in their distress and to keep oneself from being polluted by the world. (James 1:27)

Isn't that interesting? What kind of pollution is He talking about? The pollution of selfish gain. Don't be like the world, hoarding your blessings for yourself. Share your wealth. Feed others. Jesus clearly responded to Peter's claims that he loved Him with "Feed my sheep." Use both faith and material helps. Jesus could well have said, "If you love Me, please Me by doing what is important to Me. Make Me look good. Make Me desirable to those who don't know Me by making My care for them evident in your giving. Give of yourselves, give of what you have."

IT IS BETTER TO GIVE THAN TO RECEIVE

One day I was in a hurry, trying to get out of town for a speaking engagement. As I drove my car down the street, a young lady crossed my path and I almost collided with her. I was upset with her for not realizing that I had the green light. She should not have been walking across the street at that time. I wondered aloud what was the matter with her and continued to the gas station to fill up for the journey. As I got back into the car, I noticed that this same young lady had circled back to the gas station and crossed in front of my car to ask the customer in front of me for money. The person ignored her, but I felt a tug in my spirit to give her some money. I called her over to the car and gave her a twenty-dollar bill. Do you know what she said? She said, "Are you a Christian?"

"Yes," I said.

"Thank you for the money," she said, "but could you please pray for me?" Well, I began to pray over that girl right there and then as others in the gas station looked on. She went away praising God, rejoicing in the fact that He cared for her. It was a God moment. I was happy I could give her more than money, and I thought to myself as I drove off, "Truly this is what the Christian life is all about. God, grant me more opportunities like that one." He had chosen to use me as a vessel to glorify Him.

When I consider those in the world who have an abundance of wealth, most of those people make major contributions on behalf of children or the unfortunate. From people like Oprah Winfrey to Bill Gates, Christians and non-Christians alike flourish. Why? Because although they have acquired a lot of things for themselves, they are faithful in giving to others. They abide by the principle of sowing and reaping.

I was talking with a wealthy friend of mine one day, and we were discussing a designer line of clothing. I was complaining about the exorbitant prices of the articles, although I knew these things were well within my friend's reach. But then she said something that rocked my world. She said, "I agree with you, and though I love her designs I just couldn't spend God's money like that." Wow! God's money. In her mind her money did not belong to her. I have to admit I had never looked at finances in that light, but the more I thought about it, I realized her perspective was right on. I began to think of my bank account differently. God had left it in my care, and He trusted me to use it wisely. My friend and I went on to discuss being a wise steward over that which God has given us. I walked away with a greater sense of purpose and a renewed understanding of true stewardship in light of kingdom business.

IT'S ALL OR NOTHING

Looking at the life of Jesus, we see the ultimate illustration of giving everything and gaining the world. Jesus loved not His own life, but gave it willingly for the sake of others. For the sake of the kingdom. Therefore God made Him Lord over all.

> The Father loves the Son and has placed everything in his hands. (John 3:35)

Jesus was willing to be misunderstood in order to carry out the desires of the Father. A life of selflessness is not without opposition. Just as the devil confronted Jesus and tempted Him to take self-preserving measures, the enemy of your soul will come to taunt you, to tell you that you are a fool, that your giving is in vain and unappreciated. Yet you must persevere in your principal quest: to do the Father's bidding. Your efforts will not go unrewarded.

> But seek first his kingdom and his righteousness, and
> *all* these *things* will be *given* to you as well. (Matthew
> 6:33)

You must be willing to follow Jesus down the path of sacrifice in order to gain the greater blessings that await those who choose His way. Mary said yes to God knowing that it would cost her something, that it could in fact cost her everything! She had no idea how Joseph would take the news that she was pregnant, pregnant with the Son of God. How does one explain such a thing? She had to have considered that he might not believe her. If he didn't believe her, the consequences could be grave indeed. She could be accused of fornication and stoned to death. Yet sharing the angel's message was a chance she would take to birth, literally, the purposes of God. If Joseph did not choose to join her, so be it. Though it could cost her reputation, family, and all that she held dear, so be it. God's will be done above all things. She was willing to take the chance. This fierce allegiance to the purposes of God was exactly what He was looking for.

In our quest to fulfill God's call on our lives, we will likely be misunderstood along the way. We will be challenged by people to use our gifts and resources in ways other than the way God has asked of us, but we must remain true to our call in order to know the blessed life. Some might challenge your tithing. Your celibacy. Your refusal to give up on a difficult marriage. Some might challenge your sacrifice of a high-profile job for the sake of ministry. Whatever it is that causes you to be peculiar in the eyes of others, if God has called you to it, persevere in it; your reward is on the way. God is watching how you handle your circumstances. And whatever the circumstances, we must make a stand for the purposes of God. His desires must be our desires; His priorities, our priorities. When our hearts are in the right place, God can trust us to be wise stewards over what He gives—and give He will!

> Whoever can be trusted with very *little* can also be trusted with much, and whoever is dishonest with very *little* will also be dishonest with much. (Luke 16:10)

> "Well done, my good servant!" his master replied. "Because you have been trustworthy in a very small matter, take charge of ten cities." (Luke 19:17)

Yes, God is watching. Watching how you behave. Watching how you spend what you have. Watching how you spend your time. Watching what you give to others. How you handle authority. How you submit to those over you. If you can submit, God can trust you to lead. If you give out of your need, He can trust you to give out of plenty.

Are you getting the picture? If God can trust you to be a living sacrifice, proving what is His good, acceptable, and perfect will, He will take your sacrifice and exchange it for incredible blessing. Mary gave what she had to God. Herself. And she was blessed.

Thoughts to Ponder

- What motivates your decisions and choices?
- Are your aspirations good ideas or God ideas?
- What would God say about how you spend your time? Your money?
- Can God trust you with power? Money? Position?
- How do your desires fit in with kingdom business? Are you concerned about what God is concerned about?

what's in a name?

LETTING YOUR REPUTATION WORK FOR YOU

But why am I so favored, that the mother of my Lord
should come to me?

LUKE 1:43

Shakespeare wrote, "What's in a name? That which we call a rose by any other name would smell as sweet." Perhaps that's true, but names do seem to bear a lot of weight at least in our floral selections. Discriminating flower shoppers know of one rose in particular whose reputation precedes it: the American Beauty. When you want to present your best or really make a statement, a dozen of these gorgeous red flowers will always impress.

Why is a good name so important? Because it defines, simply and succinctly, who we are. When I left the ad agency I worked for, I never had to call anyone to secure work. I didn't realize how the work I'd done up to that time had set the stage for my life as a freelancer. When the buzz that I was self-employed hit the street, the phone began to ring. "So-and-so said you were just the person I needed for this project. Are you interested?" "I heard you are really good at this." "I hear you're the one to call." My name had become associated with excellence in my field, and I never even knew that anyone was paying attention! I had cultivated a good reputation in advertising circles, not because I had been networking, but because I had applied myself to being superb at my craft. This was my way of glorifying God in the workplace. When people asked me how I came up with my ideas, I'd say, "Well, I simply pray and wait for God's creativity to operate through me." Some looked at me quizzically. I'm sure they were thinking there had to be more to it than that. But believe me, there wasn't.

FIRST IMPRESSIONS ARE LASTING ONES

A good name creates favor for you and opens the door for countless blessings. This is why it is so important to always walk in righteousness and excellence. We never know who is watching us or in what situations our reputation will pave the way for promotion or demotion.

> When a man's ways are pleasing to the LORD,
>   he makes even his enemies live at peace with him.
>   (Proverbs 16:7)

When Joseph received news of Mary's pregnancy, he found himself torn. I believe the godly life she had led caused him to seek a way to protect her rather than to expose her, though he couldn't reconcile how she could be pregnant without human contact. He knew that Mary was a woman after God's own heart, a woman who would not wander beyond the righteous boundaries of God's law. Therefore his heart was open to instruction from the angel who confirmed that, indeed, Mary's pregnancy was a holy event and that Joseph should proceed with his marriage plans.

After he had considered this, an angel of the Lord appeared to him in a dream and said, "Joseph son of David, do not be afraid to take Mary home as your wife, because what is conceived in her is from the Holy Spirit. She will give birth to a son, and you are to give him the name Jesus, because he will save his people from their sins."

All this took place to fulfill what the Lord had said through the prophet: "The virgin will be with child and will give birth to a son, and they will call him Immanuel"—which means, "God with us."

When Joseph woke up, he did what the angel of the Lord had commanded him and took Mary home as his wife. (Matthew 1:20-24)

Now that's what a good name will do for you! Mary had lived a faultless life before God, so the insinuations of the enemy were not able to stick to her. God came to her defense, and Joseph rose to the occasion by standing beside her as her covering and husband.

My son, do not forget my teaching,
 but keep my commands in your heart,
for they will prolong your life many years
 and bring you prosperity.
Let love and faithfulness never leave you;
 bind them around your neck,
 write them on the tablet of your heart.
Then you will win favor and a good name
 in the sight of God and man. (Proverbs 3:1-4)

When God is on your side, what can man do to you? Who can say no to you when God says yes? A clean conscience and right-standing with God are the prerequisites for a sparkling reputation and a good name. If you want a good long life and prosperity, cultivate a good name.

> A *good name* is more desirable than great riches;
>   to be esteemed is better than silver or gold.
>   (Proverbs 22:1)

> A *good name* is better than fine perfume.
>   (Ecclesiastes 7:1)

A good name cannot be spent, it will not tarnish, and, like perfume, it lingers long after you've left the room. Have you ever been in a room with someone who has on a wonderful fragrance? When he or she leaves, the memory of that person remains with you. You almost want to follow in order to continue the pleasant experience. Like that kind of perfume, our name should bring a smile to the faces of God and man when mentioned. And when people think highly of you, they are willing to extend a favor on your behalf.

THE BENEFITS OF HEARSAY

Ruth was minding her own business, gleaning in the fields of Boaz, when she caught his eye. When he inquired after her identity, her good name spoke on her behalf, and he made special concessions to make sure she had what she needed.

At this, she bowed down with her face to the ground. She exclaimed, "Why have I found such favor in your eyes that you notice me—a foreigner?"

Boaz replied, "I've been told all about what you have done for your mother-in-law since the death of your husband—how you left your father and mother and your homeland and came to live with a people you did not know before. May the LORD repay you for what you have done. May you be richly rewarded by the LORD, the God of Israel, under whose wings you have come to take refuge."

"May I continue to find favor in your eyes, my lord," she said. "You have given me comfort and have spoken kindly to your servant—though I do not have the standing of one of your servant girls." (Ruth 2:10-13)

There is no deep spiritual principle here, just good godly sense. Notice I didn't say common sense because sense is not common. When people think highly of you, they will do good for you, even when others accuse you of wrongdoing.

I think of Jacob's son Joseph, accused of rape by Mrs. Potiphar. Due to the integrity that Joseph had always displayed to Potiphar, Joseph had a good name. Oh, in order to keep the peace at home, Potiphar had to address what his wife had told him, but he could not get past what he knew to be true of Joseph. So Potiphar put Joseph in the king's prison instead of ordering the usual death penalty for such a crime. And it was Potiphar who placed the Pharaoh's wine steward and chief baker under Joseph's care in the prison. These two events, plus Joseph's ability to tap into the spirit of

God and interpret these men's dreams, gained him release from prison and promotion to the right-hand man of the Pharaoh of Egypt.

MAKING A NAME FOR YOURSELF

Even the heathens knew the importance of names. When Daniel went into the employ of the king of Babylon, the king changed Daniel's name to Belteshazzar, after a Babylonian god. But Daniel held fast to his Hebrew name, refusing to change the confession of faith that it was. I find it interesting that despite his name change everyone still continued to call him Daniel!—so great was his stand and lack of compromise. Because of his excellent service to the king, no one bothered to dispute him. Daniel (meaning "God is my judge") survived four administrations of Babylonian government because of his good name.

Now think about how unusual that is. Governments and corporations are famous for cleaning house whenever a new leader comes on the scene. Newcomers usually clear out the old administration and bring in all of their own people. But Daniel's reputation for wisdom and integrity preceded him. Incoming kings actually chose Daniel for chief administrative services. King Darius, the third king Daniel served, was so impressed with Daniel that he placed him over the entire empire. Of course this did not sit well with the other administrators and princes at all.

> Now Daniel so distinguished himself among the administrators and the satraps by his exceptional qualities that the king planned to set him over the whole king-

dom. At this, the administrators and the satraps tried to find grounds for charges against Daniel in his conduct of government affairs, but they were unable to do so. They could find no corruption in him, because he was trustworthy and neither corrupt nor negligent. Finally these men said, "We will never find any basis for charges against this man Daniel unless it has something to do with the law of his God." (Daniel 6:3-5)

So they conspired against Daniel and devised a law against prayer that they knew he would break. Everyone knew Daniel was a praying man. So they bamboozled the king into writing a decree against prayer. Then they lay in wait.

When they caught Daniel offering his usual supplications to the Lord, they were quick to run and report him to the king. But an unusual thing happened.

When the king heard this, he was greatly distressed; he was determined to rescue Daniel and made every effort until sundown to save him.

Then the men went as a group to the king and said to him, "Remember, O king, that according to the law of the Medes and Persians no decree or edict that the king issues can be changed." So the king gave the order, and they brought Daniel and threw him into the lions' den. The king said to Daniel, "May your God, whom you serve continually, rescue you!" (Daniel 6:14-16)

Now when you are known as a man or a woman who continually serves God, guess what? God's name is on the line too. And you had better believe God is able to show up and show Himself to be strong on your behalf. He will move the hearts of those who opposed you and set you up for victory. He will have those who opposed you cheering you on. He Himself will come down and be your buckler and your shield, your strong defense. He will grant you the power to be an overcomer despite the circumstances. That's just a natural part of the blessed life.

> Then the king returned to his palace and spent the night without eating and without any entertainment being brought to him. And he could not sleep.
>
> At the first light of dawn, the king got up and hurried to the lions' den. When he came near the den, he called to Daniel in an anguished voice, "Daniel, servant of the living God, has your God, whom you serve continually, been able to rescue you from the lions?"
>
> Daniel answered, "O king, live forever! My God sent his angel, and he shut the mouths of the lions. They have not hurt me, because I was found innocent in his sight. Nor have I ever done any wrong before you, O king."
>
> The king was overjoyed and gave orders to lift Daniel out of the den. And when Daniel was lifted from the den, no wound was found on him, because he had trusted in his God.
>
> At the king's command, the men who had falsely accused Daniel were brought in and thrown into the

lions' den, along with their wives and children. And before they reached the floor of the den, the lions over-powered them and crushed all their bones.

Then King Darius wrote to all the peoples, nations and men of every language throughout the land:

"May you prosper greatly!

"I issue a decree that in every part of my kingdom people must fear and reverence the God of Daniel.

"For he is the living God
   and he endures forever;
his kingdom will not be destroyed,
   his dominion will never end.
He rescues and he saves;
   he performs signs and wonders
   in the heavens and on the earth.
He has rescued Daniel
   from the power of the lions."

So Daniel prospered during the reign of Darius and the reign of Cyrus the Persian. (Daniel 6:18-28)

See what I mean? A good name is powerful, more powerful than bribe money or anything else you could think of to use as leverage in the natural world. Your good name will cause people to praise God's name. Why? Because they can see the evidence of Him at work in your life as you seek to honor Him in all that you do.

IT'S ALL IN A NAME

In the end our names or our reputations are really all we have that completely represents who we are. Our name encapsulates our personal legacy, which will remain to speak of our character and integrity long after we have departed. This is why God chooses to swear by His own name.

> When God made his promise to Abraham, since there
> was no one greater for him to swear by, he *swore* by
> *himself.* (Hebrews 6:13)

Our name is our confession. What we confess is what we are. Our words have power. The power of death and life is in our tongues, according to the book of James. That's why I always urge those I know to be careful what they name their children. My name, *Michelle,* means "Who is like God?" That is, "one who stands behind and practices absolute truth." My middle name, *Ayodele,* means, "Joy arrives in the home." Now those are two good daily confessions for my life. They keep me remembering the call of God on my life. Every time someone calls my name, that person reinforces my identity and God's call: "Hey, you who stands behind and practices absolute truth, you who carries joy—how are you today?" I've got to line up my life with that because, with the pronouncement of my name, the air is charged with who I am supposed to be and how I am supposed to live!

Psychologists have found that children with unusual names are more prone to juvenile delinquency because they are constantly teased about their names. I would dare to go a step further and add the spiritual implication that, if a child's name doesn't mean anything, he or she will be more likely to have a sense of meaninglessness that provokes him or her to cause trouble.

God deliberately chose to name those who would be instrumental in His plan. The given names described the character and attributes of the man or woman God had chosen. At times the Lord changed an individual's name because a transformation had taken place in that person's life. Abram (exalted father) was changed to Abraham (father of many nations). Sarai (princess) became Sarah (noblewoman), and Jacob (supplanter), Israel (prince). These people had come into the fullness of what God had called them to be and were identified as such.

Since no single name is sufficient to describe God, He chose to call Himself "I Am," because He is all things. Even Jesus could not be described by just one name.

> Behold, a virgin shall be with child, and shall bring forth a son, and they shall call his name Emmanuel which being interpreted is, God with us. (Matthew 1:23, KJV)

> For unto us a child is born, unto us a son is given: and the government shall be upon his shoulder: and his name shall be called Wonderful, Counsellor, The mighty God, The everlasting Father, The Prince of Peace. (Isaiah 9:6, KJV)

Isn't that incredible? God is so many things that He requires a myriad of names. Think of all the things we call Him: Jehovah Jireh (our provider),

Jehovah Shalom (He is our peace), Abba Father, Yahweh. And that's just the beginning of all His names! Each of these describes but one feature of many belonging to our complex God, who encompasses more than we will ever be able to imagine. And still He is our loving Father. Our God. Our King. Our confidence is in His name because it is the embodiment of what He has promised to be for us.

> I will praise you forever for what you have done;
>   in your *name* I will hope, for your *name* is *good.*
>   I will praise you in the presence of your saints.
>   (Psalm 52:9)

> I will sacrifice a freewill offering to you;
>   I will praise your *name,* O Lord,
>   for it is *good.* (Psalm 54:6)

There is authority in the name of Jesus because He has been proclaimed Lord and King. We are able to stand firm before the enemy of our souls because we have the assurance that at the name of Jesus, all things must come into submission to His Lordship. In other words, He has our back!

> Therefore God exalted him to the highest place
>   and gave him the name that is above every name,
>   that at the name of Jesus every knee should bow,
>   in heaven and on earth and under the earth,
>   and every tongue confess that Jesus Christ is Lord,
>   to the glory of God the Father. (Philippians 2:9-11)

God's name proclaims His sovereignty. What does your name proclaim about you? The mere mention of certain names elicits a quick response: awe, respect, laughter, disdain. Our hearts open or shut at the sound of a person's name.

When others hear your name, do you think the words *faithful, honest, responsible, loving, kind,* and *dependable* come to their minds?

Consider someone like Jacob, whose name meant "supplanter." He connived his way through the early years of his life, but his true identity caught up with him when he needed a blessing from God. "What is your name?" God asked him. Jacob had to confess who he truly was, a supplanter, and only then did God change his name and transform him into a man of honor. Jacob became Israel, "prince," and the father of the tribes of that nation which would affect the world for all eternity. Wow! If our names have been tarnished, truly God is able to redeem our past failures and ruined reputations as we come clean with Him, allowing Him to wash us and make us new creations in Him. He is willing to do so because He fully understands the importance of a good name.

The reaction people have to your name can affect your blessings. That's why this discussion of names brings us full circle to our relationship with God. Do you walk in a godly fashion and, by so doing, place yourself in right standing with God and others? Favor with God affects your favor with man. You need that favor for open doors, for effectual opportunities to prosper in your calling and giftings. You need that favor in order to be blessed. You see, part of the secret of getting blessed is giving your heavenly Father something to work with. Why not start with a good name? Mary had a good name. It gave her favor with God and with Joseph, and she was blessed.

Thoughts to Ponder

- What does your name mean? Are you the embodiment of your name? Do you take your name's confession over your life seriously?
- How do you think people respond when they hear your name?
- What standards have you set for yourself in order to cultivate a godly reputation?
- Do people know that you are a Christian even when you don't tell them?
- What is the one descriptive word you would like placed by your name if it were in the dictionary?

a word in time

UNDERSTANDING THE POWER OF SILENCE

But *Mary* treasured up all these things and *pondered*
them in her heart.

LUKE 2:19

When God speaks, the universe listens. But sometimes He speaks only
to you.

Can you keep a secret? Sometimes being able to keep a secret is important to receiving God's blessings. Let me explain by first asking a question.
Have you ever been promised a great deal by someone and been so excited
about it that you just had to tell everybody? I'll bet everybody wanted to
know why they weren't getting the same deal, and they started raising sand
about it. What happened? Either your deal got put on hold until the furor
died down, or it was withdrawn completely in order to keep the peace.

Words spoken out of season can get us in trouble. Sometimes you have
to keep to yourself the details of those great and wonderful promises,
whether from God or someone else, until the appointed time. Remember,
we are partners with God in this blessing thing. You can make it easy, or
you can make it more difficult than it has to be.

Not everyone is going to be happy about the things God has promised you. Satan certainly won't be. He will raise his ugly head to question you and try to dislodge your faith. Others will be just plain jealous because God didn't promise them the same thing. People who wait on God's promises may be viewed as unrealistic dreamers. And people don't like dreamers. Dreamers make people uncomfortable, perhaps because dreamers expose a lack of vision and a sense of purposelessness that other people may be feeling. Joseph found this out the hard way.

> Now Israel loved Joseph more than any of his other sons, because he had been born to him in his old age; and he made a richly ornamented robe for him. When his brothers saw that their father loved him more than any of them, they hated him and could not speak a kind word to him.
>
> Joseph had a dream, and when he told it to his brothers, they hated him all the more. (Genesis 37:3-5)

You know the rest of the story. The brothers focused on Joseph's dream even more than he did, I think, and they were so incensed that they sought his harm.

> Then he had another dream, and he told it to his brothers. "Listen," he said, "I had another dream...."
>
> When he told his father as well as his brothers, his father rebuked him and said, "What is this dream you had?..." [Joseph's] brothers were jealous of him....

They saw him in the distance, and before he reached
them, they plotted to kill him.

"Here comes that dreamer!" they said to each other.
"Come now, let's kill him and throw him into one of
these cisterns and say that a ferocious animal devoured
him. Then we'll see what comes of his dreams." (Genesis 37:9-11,18-20)

Joseph had spoken too soon. Although he didn't know it, his dreams would
not be realized for years. Now, mind you, God used the evil plot of Joseph's
brothers to position Joseph exactly where he needed to be in order for his
dream to be fulfilled. We will never know how God would have gotten
him to Egypt any other way, but that's beside the point. The bottom line is
that sometimes we bring unnecessary complications into our lives by speaking out of time. I find it interesting that when his dreams were fulfilled,
Joseph wasn't as quick to reveal his identity to his brothers. He had learned
a thing or two about timing.

Even God doesn't tell us everything at once. Although He already
knows all the details of our lives, He gives us only as much as He knows we
can handle at any given time. Too much information at the wrong time is
not a good thing. It leaves too much room for error, misunderstanding, confusion, and strife of various kinds. Sometimes you just have to keep things to
yourself until they come into full manifestation. The enemy of your soul will
use others to try to steal, kill, and destroy the dream God has placed in your
life. Even after the dream has been birthed, he keeps on trying! But we can
sometimes prevent the abortion of God's dreams by learning how to hold
our words for the right season.

There is a time for everything,

> and a season for every activity under heaven:…

> a time to be silent and a time to speak.…

> He has made everything beautiful in its time. He has also set eternity in the hearts of men; yet they cannot fathom what God has done from beginning to end. (Ecclesiastes 3:1,7,11)

The eyes of all look to you,

> and you give them their food at the proper time.

You open your hand

> and satisfy the desires of every living thing.

> > (Psalm 145:15-16)

Many of us are so quick to blab it and grab it that we end up grabbing the wrong thing. The opinions of others misguide us. Therefore, it is best to quietly wait on the Lord.

Now that word *wait* is not a passive word. Waiting can be quite active. Wait on the Lord to take care of what He said while you delight yourself in serving Him. Keep moving forward toward His promise. Do what it takes to be in position to receive His blessing. The best position to be in is as close to God as you can get, right smack dab in the center of His will, doing what He's called you to do. You take care of His business and He will take care of yours. God tells us secrets so we will draw closer to Him to hear and see the rest, not so we will burst into action trying to bring about what He has spoken or to convince others of what He said. The proof will be in the pudding soon enough.

WHAT YOU SAY IS WHAT YOU GET?

Truly the power of life and death is in the tongue. Have you ever shared a secret longing with others only to have them destroy your hopes? They spoke doubt and death to your dream. They took the joy out of it and killed it for you. Perhaps you walked away resolved to no longer pursue your dream. You convinced yourself that what they said made sense. You disregarded the power of God to do the impossible. Small wonder that, when it comes to those things crucial to God's purposes, He will take drastic measures to prevent the vision from fading. He knows what our mouths do; therefore He will either not tell us what He is going to do, or He will arrest us by His Spirit to keep what He has spoken under wraps. We must be sensitive to the leading of the Spirit when this occurs, recognizing the right moment to speak up.

When the angel told Zechariah, the husband of Mary's cousin, Elizabeth, that they would have a son in their old age who would be the forerunner of Jesus, the poor old man had a hard time believing.

> Zechariah asked the angel, "How can I be sure of this? I am an old man and my wife is well along in years."
>
> The angel answered, "I am Gabriel. I stand in the presence of God, and I have been sent to speak to you and to tell you this good news. And now you will be silent and not able to speak until the day this happens, because you did not believe my words, which will come true at their proper time."
>
> Meanwhile, the people were waiting for Zechariah and wondering why he stayed so long in the temple.

When he came out, he could not speak to them. They realized he had seen a vision in the temple, for he kept making signs to them but remained unable to speak....

When it was time for Elizabeth to have her baby, she gave birth to a son....

On the eighth day they came to circumcise the child, and they were going to name him after his father Zechariah, but his mother spoke up and said, "No! He is to be called John."

They said to her, "There is no one among your relatives who has that name."

Then they made signs to his father, to find out what he would like to name the child. He asked for a writing tablet, and to everyone's astonishment he wrote, "His name is John." Immediately his mouth was opened and his tongue was loosed, and he began to speak, praising God. (Luke 1:18-22,57,59-64)

How's that for keeping a person out of the way? Zechariah was not able to speak until he was able to confess the Word of God about the matter. Notice that Elizabeth had no problem aligning herself with God's chosen name for the baby. She was adamant and would not be moved by the crowd.

If you must share what God has revealed to you, make sure you choose someone who is able to match your faith. As inspiring minister Tim Story says, "Look for your Elizabeth." Mary knew whom to seek out when she was overwhelmed with her miraculous situation. She sought out the companionship and encouragement of Elizabeth, and Elizabeth was able to exhort Mary because she was experiencing her own miracle!

You've got to have someone in your life who is able to relate to your experience and partner with you in faith. Those who have not been where you're going will have difficulty finding the path and urging you onward. They will be unable to appreciate your experience.

KEEPING IT UNDER WRAPS

To share your dream or promise with someone who has no concept of the miraculous is like casting your pearls before swine. Expect no words of encouragement or any other good thing. Those who have not experienced the favor of God will not be able to join you in faith. In fact, they will downright hurt your feelings.

> Do not give dogs what is sacred; do not throw your *pearls*
> to pigs. If you do, they may trample them under their
> feet, and then turn and tear you to pieces. (Matthew 7:6)

Mm-hm, they'll trample your dream and not be satisfied to do just that. They will add insult to injury by telling you that you think more highly of yourself than you ought. That you're being a bit too "high sa-diddy" (that's "uppity" in urbanese). After all, why should God bless you like that when they haven't been blessed that way? Well, the answer to that is simply, "Because I expect more from God." Or even better, because you've been working to apply principles to your life that put you in line for a blessing.

So again I say, if you just *must* tell somebody, make sure it's someone who can handle the information in a godly fashion. Even so, God will sometimes require you to do as Mary did and ponder what He has told you in your heart. Even if others receive a witness in their heart concerning God's promise to you and they confirm what has been resting in your spirit, even then continue to guard it.

> And there were shepherds living out in the fields nearby, keeping watch over their flocks at night. An angel of the Lord appeared to them, and the glory of the Lord shone around them, and they were terrified. But the angel said to them, "Do not be afraid. I bring you good news of great joy that will be for all the people. Today in the town of David a Savior has been born to you; he is Christ the Lord. This will be a sign to you: You will find a baby wrapped in cloths and lying in a manger."...
>
> When the angels had left them and gone into heaven, the shepherds said to one another, "Let's go to Bethlehem and see this thing that has happened, which the Lord has told us about."
>
> So they hurried off and found Mary and Joseph, and the baby, who was lying in the manger. When they had seen him, they spread the word concerning what had been told them about this child, and all who heard it were amazed at what the shepherds said to them. But Mary treasured up all these things and pondered them in her heart. (Luke 2:8-12,15-19)

When God has spoken a word to you, He will send others to confirm it. Allow Him to select those people. They will be people who are in the Spirit. They will be people who anxiously await the fulfillment of God's agenda, not their own. They are not selfish or self-consumed. The desires of God matter most to them. Their will is lost inside His; therefore, they are not inclined to think negatively about a person who is being set up for promotion or a blessing. They keep kingdom business in full view, seeing it as a blessing for the body and not for just one individual.

> Now there was a man in Jerusalem called Simeon, who was righteous and devout. He was waiting for the consolation of Israel, and the Holy Spirit was upon him. It had been revealed to him by the Holy Spirit that he would not die before he had seen the Lord's Christ. Moved by the Spirit, he went into the temple courts. When the parents brought in the child Jesus to do for him what the custom of the Law required, Simeon took him in his arms and praised God, saying,
>
> "Sovereign Lord, as you have promised,
>   you now dismiss your servant in peace.
> For my eyes have seen your salvation,
>   which you have prepared in the sight of all people,
> a light for revelation to the Gentiles
>   and for glory to your people Israel."
>
> The child's father and mother marveled at what was said about him. (Luke 2:25-33)

When God has spoken, many of us are not confident that we have heard *His* voice. We seek validation and find ourselves as invalids instead, paralyzed by the unbelief or disdain of others. But God will select an unselfish encourager for you. One who knows how to pray and to travail with you until the time for the manifestation of the promise is upon you. When you are believing for the incredible, extraordinary blessings of God, chances are you're going to have a long labor in the birthing process. You need a spiritual midwife to coach you through, to tell you when to wait and when to push.

BIRTHING THE VISION

If you've ever seen a mother in her eighth or ninth month of pregnancy, you may have heard "I am ready for this baby to come out!" That woman has carried and incubated that child to the birthing point, and now she's ready to deliver it. But guess what? That child isn't coming out until he or she is good and ready!

God's blessings and promises are like that. Others who induce labor for whatever reason typically find that the pain of the delivery process is intensified. Their bodies are unprepared for delivery, and it is literally a shock to the system. The body is hostile to the disturbance. When we try to make things happen either through our actions or the things we say, I believe it sends shock waves through the spirit realm that cause unnecessary tension or pressure. Our efforts will affect people negatively because we are out of order. But the mother—as well as the servant of God—who simply lets nature take its course, though not escaping pain, fares better than the one who induced the delivery.

Prosperity theologies may have added fuel to this fire. These urge Christians to "name it, claim it, and frame it." They say that confession is everything, and if you can't confess it, you can't get it. We must find the balance in this line of thinking. What we must confess daily is *who God is and what He is able to do,* not the specific expectation of blessing, because that type of confession puts God in a box of our own making. And He will not abide there. After all, what if He wants to do more than you're confessing?

Jesus spoke constantly of the Father, His abilities, and the things that were already established in the heavenlies. Then He opened His hands and simply watched for God to move in any way He desired. Of course, Jesus was so close to His Father that He knew the specifics of what the Almighty would do. At the appropriate time the Lord's plans would be revealed. Until then, however, Jesus tucked the details away in His heart until every piece was in place, set in position for the fulfillment of what God had decreed. Then Jesus released it, giving life to the promise. When we wait on the Lord for the birthing of blessings, we will echo those in the book of Acts on the day of Pentecost who said, "This is what was spoken of…" (2:16, NASB).

TIMING IS EVERYTHING

God waits to reveal His plans. He is not willing to be interrupted or circumvented by either our flesh or the natural urge we have to make things happen. Throughout the Old Testament He gives us glimpses of a Savior. But after the Savior bursts onto the scene, He reveals yet another aspect of His plan: to invite Gentiles into the lineage of Abraham, Isaac, and Jacob. We get hints of this intention in the Old Testament, but in the New Testament God lays it out plainly through the life and writings of Paul. Paul is God's Elizabeth, ready to partner with Him in this undertaking.

In reading this, then, you will be able to understand my insight into the mystery of Christ, which was not made known to men in other generations as it has now been revealed by the Spirit to God's holy apostles and prophets. This mystery is that through the gospel the Gentiles are heirs together with Israel, members together of one body, and sharers together in the promise in Christ Jesus....

Although I am less than the least of all God's people, this grace was given me: to preach to the Gentiles the unsearchable riches of Christ, and to make plain to everyone the administration of this mystery, which for ages past was kept hidden in God, who created all things. His intent was that now, through the church, the manifold wisdom of God should be made known to the rulers and authorities in the heavenly realms, according to his eternal purpose which he accomplished in Christ Jesus our Lord. (Ephesians 3:4-6,8-11)

Can God keep a secret or what? From the beginning God was plotting and planning the salvation of the *world,* giving hints along the way that could not be fully comprehended. I have this picture in my mind of all the angels in heaven saying, "What is God up to? What is He doing? Why is the Lamb going down to earth? Why is God allowing His Son to be killed? What is this all about?" Then all of a sudden—*bam!* The entire picture is revealed. Christ dies, is resurrected, and ascends back to heaven with the keys of death and hell in His hands. And all of heaven has one giant "Ah! Now I see!" moment. Satan couldn't mess up the plan because, for one thing, He didn't even know it. God didn't utter a word, He just did His thing, and now we are all blessed because of it. We have favor because of the blood of Jesus. As many a preacher has said, if Satan had known what the crucifixion would have accomplished, he would never have had Jesus killed. Remember, silence is your friend. A word out of season can be your worst enemy and rob you of your blessing.

The book of Nehemiah documents Nehemiah's return to Jerusalem to rebuild its wall. After securing written documentation that confirmed his right to proceed, he set out to do what God had laid on his heart. With wise foresight, he had chosen to keep his plans to himself until he arrived. He traveled by night to inspect the ruins and, after surveying and estimating the extent of the work to be done, met with the leaders to outline a strategy. By the time Jerusalem's enemies got wind of what was happening, it was too late. The plans were already underway, and their opposition was thwarted.

So do you feel like you will just burst with anticipation of what God is going to do in your life? If He said it, He will do it. So for your own sake, before you explode, write it down. The written word has power and is subject to no one.

Then the Lord replied:

"Write down the revelation
    and make it plain on tablets
    so that a herald may run with it.
For the revelation awaits an appointed time;
    it speaks of the end
    and will not prove false.

Though it linger, wait for it;

it will certainly come and will not delay."

(Habakkuk 2:2-3)

For no word from God shall be void of power. (Luke 1:37, ASV)

Seek validation and confirmation only from the Spirit of God. When He is the One who has spoken the promise, He will surely bring it to pass. The gates of hell cannot prevail against the blessings He has stored up for you, but waiting wisely for their delivery is key. Mary didn't run around screaming to the world, "My baby is the Son of God, and He's going to save everybody!" No, she rested in the knowledge of the things that had been told to her, pondering them in her heart, and she was blessed.

Thoughts to Ponder

- What has God promised you? Do you believe Him?
- What instructions has He given you concerning the promise? Are you actively pursuing Him for more instruction?
- Can God trust you with His secrets?
- Do you trust God to deliver what He has promised?
- Are you willing to wait on the delivery of God's promise? What steps of preparation will you take?
- Are you willing to do the work to birth God's promise when the time comes? To what extent?

the power of submission

LEARNING HOW TO GET TO THE TOP

And Mary said:
"My soul glorifies the Lord
and my spirit rejoices in God my Savior,
for he has been mindful
of the humble state of his servant."

LUKE 1:46-48

I sat and listened to my friend express her disappointment. "God has never blessed me," she said. The words sent chills down my spine. I stifled the urge to reply, "How can you say that? You are sitting before me in perfect health. You are not homeless. We just finished a fabulous lunch. How could you put your lips together to utter such a thing?" But because I was cognizant of the pain that had forced these words out of the basement of her heart, I remained silent, waiting until a better time to speak reason to her. For now I would allow her to feel what she felt without feeling judged as well.

My friend's disappointment was real. It could not be denied, and yet I had a different perspective on her life. I saw before me someone I loved very much who was writhing in her own self-involvement. Her life had always been about what she wanted from God, never about what God wanted from her. And so God waited for her to give her heart to Him so that He could fill it. I wonder why it wasn't clear to her that she was her own worst enemy. I knew she had dreams she had never pursued because she was unwilling to commit to doing the extra work required to gain the extra-dimensional blessings of God. Yet she desired them and felt *entitled* to them. But a basic life only gets us the basic blessings at best. Now was not the time for me to share these observations with her. There's a time for everything, including loving correction.

I walked away questioning myself and the condition of my own heart. Did I regard God as a sort of Santa Claus? Or was He more like a slot machine? If I put in a token of obedience, would I expect a prize to automatically drop into my hands? Depending on our own experiences with our earthly father, other men, or authority figures in our lives, our view of our heavenly Father may be limited and incorrect. Our experience might be as basic as "If I do this, you will reward me with that"—Pavlov's dog theory on a human level.

But God doesn't practice behavior modification techniques with us. We cannot manipulate Him. To feel that we are here for our own benefit and that God exists to give us the desires of our heart will get us nowhere fast in the blessing department.

> Thou art worthy, O Lord, to receive glory and honour
> and power: for thou hast *created* all things, and for thy
> *pleasure* they are and were *created*. (Revelation 4:11, KJV)

We have to remember that we are here *for God*. For *His* purposes and *His* pleasure. As we bring pleasure to His heart, He opens the windows of heaven and pours out more blessings than we have room to receive. From our hearts to our tithes to our talents to our time, all that we are and all that we have belongs to the Lord. Mary was willing to give God the use of her life, no matter what it might cost her: the wrath of Joseph, the misunderstanding and judgment of her family and community, the loss of freedom that having a child would bring, *her very future.* She put aside her personal desires to fulfill the will of the Father. She was willing to do the work that the call on her life required come pain, shame, or lack of free time…whatever! She was up to the task. That is the heart of a true servant, a servant who is destined to be blessed above the norm.

> Therefore, I urge you, brothers, in view of God's mercy,
> to offer your bodies as *living* sacrifices, holy and pleas-
> ing to God—this is your spiritual act of worship.
> (Romans 12:1)

Someone once said that the only problem with a living sacrifice is that it keeps crawling off the altar. But a true living sacrifice is one that is living and breathing unto God and is dead to its own desires. When we wipe clean the slate of our lives, erasing our own agenda, and allow God to write what He wants on the board, we enter into what I call the eye-has-not-seen, ear-has-not-heard, neither-has-it-entered-into-the-hearts-of-man-the-things-that-God-has-prepared-for-him zone. In short, we enter the above-all-you-can-ask-or-imagine dimension. You have let God out of the box of your assumptions. The extra-dimensional blessings are not for the lazy, the faint at heart, or the selfish.

When we take the focus off of ourselves and redirect it toward Him, God shows up and performs extraordinarily. When we let Him out of our box, He brings us boxes of His own filled with delights and incredible surprises. But these special gifts are reserved for those who are more enthralled with the Giver than the gifts. These special treats are reserved for those who put His wishes above their own. They have surrendered their will to embrace His and to all that His will requires of them.

> Delight yourself in the LORD
>> and he will give you the *desires* of your *heart.*
>> (Psalm 37:4)

> "If you keep your feet from breaking the Sabbath
>> and from doing *as you please* on my holy day,
> if you call the Sabbath a delight
>> and the LORD'S holy day honorable,
> and if you honor it by not going your own way
>> and *not doing as you please* or speaking idle words,
> then you will find your joy in the LORD,
>> and I will cause you to ride on the heights of the land
>> and to feast on the inheritance of your father Jacob."

The mouth of the LORD has spoken. (Isaiah 58:13-14)

Time and time again the promises of God are clearly stated: As we seek to give God joy, by being busy about the furtherance of His plan, by using our abilities to be His hands at work in the earth to fulfill the needs of others, then the reward of our self-sacrifice will be receiving the desires of our hearts. And let me remind you that as we lose ourselves in pleasing Him our desires change. They are transformed to match His desires for us because we are finally able to rest in the knowledge that He knows what is best for us. And trust me, we're not talking about oatmeal here! He knows what will bring us complete satisfaction.

It is the blessing of the LORD that makes rich,
and He adds no sorrow to it. (Proverbs 10:22, NASB)

I love the title of C. S. Lewis's book *Surprised by Joy.* That pretty much sums it up. I am learning more and more that I am not aware of what would really make me happy. As I survey the life that the Lord has given me and the things that now bring me the most joy, I am forced to admit that none of those things was on my original wish list. Fancy that! Who would have thunk it? Indeed, the Creator knows what would make His creation the happiest. But we have to get ourselves out of the way in order to receive this revelation.

THE HEART OF A SERVANT

Think about how you feel when you've received good service at a restaurant. When your server has paid extra attention to the details of your meal and your comfort. You want to leave a good tip to show your appreciation. On the other hand, if you had lousy service, you are probably tempted to leave a little *written* tip saying, "When you give better service, you'll get the type of tip you like." Instead, you'll probably leave something out of obligation, but not what you would have given if you had been served well.

What is considered good service? I find it interesting that the biblical kings surrounded themselves with eunuchs. Though castrating the men they drafted for service seems cruel, I think there was more to it than removing the temptations of the harem. The thought was that eunuchs would have no personal drives or desires of their own. Therefore, their entire focus would be serving and pleasing the king. They would anticipate the desires of the king and serve him without any agenda of their own. They would serve without thought of reward. They would not be distracted by the pull of their own flesh, which had been put to death. They would live only to be in the presence of the king.

When I visit my father in Ghana, West Africa, the house stewards illustrate this kind of service. Upon my arrival, I find my room prepared. The air conditioner is on, the room has been sprayed for mosquitoes and the linens are turned down. In the morning when I go downstairs, my breakfast has already been started; they've heard me stirring. I sit at the table and out it comes—all of my favorite morning fare. The cook knows what I like. Once I overheard the steward telling him to go easy on the pepper because I don't like a lot of it. The entire time I'm there I am surrounded by people who seek to make my stay enjoyable. They look out for me. They anticipate my needs and seek my comfort. If I try to lift a finger to iron a dress or do anything domestic, I am quickly shooed away with the words, "Oh no, madam, I will do that."

By now you're probably wondering why I come back home. I wonder that sometimes myself, but back to the point: I am served well. I am humbled by their giving attitude, and I always make sure that I give them good gifts before I leave. They are always grateful, but I know that their service is not based on the anticipation of a reward. It is because they take their positions of service seriously and they have a heart focused toward me. They miss me when I'm gone and await my return with gladness.

This gives me insight into the heart of God and what moves Him to bless us. God looks for the heart of the eunuch in us, and He makes generous promises to those who put aside their own desires to seek His pleasure. This means pressing past what our flesh views as inconvenient or uncomfortable. Anyone who has died to any life of his own for the sake of the one he serves is a servant in the truest sense.

For this is what the LORD says:

"To the eunuchs who keep my Sabbaths,
   who choose what pleases me
   and hold fast to my covenant—
to them I will give within my temple and its walls
   a memorial and a name
   better than sons and daughters;
I will give them an everlasting name
   that will not be cut off." (Isaiah 56:4-5)

Better than sons and daughters! Do you see that?! Surely that is favor—a name that represents carte blanche for now and eternity! Yet it seems difficult for us to accept that only when we release everything do we truly gain everything.

As Jonah sat in the belly of the whale, he came to the conclusion that "those who cling to worthless idols forfeit the grace that could be theirs" (Jonah 2:8). As I take note of those people in Scripture who prospered and were blessed mightily, one theme rings true: They all had a do-or-die mentality. They were willing to risk it all to attain a greater prize. They were willing to let go of the familiar in many cases, do what they did not want to do, press past their comfort level, and risk what they did not know in order to see what God would do.

WINNER TAKES ALL

God called Abraham out from a place where he was settled, well-off, and respected and then instructed him to go to a place he had never been. By blind faith, Abraham chose to forsake all. He followed the finger of God and became a very wealthy man, the father of many nations, and one of the pillars in the hall of faith. Lot, who went with him, did not fare as well. He did not have the heart of a servant. While his attitude should have been to follow Abraham, serve him, and develop the same type of relationship he had with God, Lot's self-centeredness soon eclipsed his call. Asking Abraham to give him a plot of land so that he could pursue his own well-being, he set off on a path that led to his undoing. Abraham had to rescue him a couple times. Who was serving whom here? Who got blessed? Abraham, of course.

On the other hand, Lot's home was destroyed, and his wife was turned to a pillar of salt. To add further injury to all of this, his own daughters seduced him in his sleep! (They had learned this type of behavior in the land Lot had chosen.) This incestuous moment gave birth to the Moabites and Ammonites, who later became enemies of Israel. A self-serving attitude always leads to destruction.

In sharp contrast to Lot is the example provided by the life of Elijah the prophet and his trainee Elisha (2 Kings 2). Elisha wanted the anointing that rested on Elijah and was willing to go the extra mile to get it. Now Elijah was training a whole company of prophets, but Elisha was the only one who pressed past the basic requirements to gain an extra portion.

> Then Elijah said to him, "Stay here; the LORD has sent
> me to the Jordan."

And he replied, "As surely as the LORD lives and as you live, I will not leave you." So the two of them walked on.

Fifty men of the company of the prophets went and stood at a distance, facing the place where Elijah and Elisha had stopped at the Jordan. Elijah took his cloak, rolled it up and struck the water with it. The water divided to the right and to the left, and the two of them crossed over on dry ground.

When they had crossed, Elijah said to Elisha, "Tell me, what can I do for you before I am taken from you?"

"Let me inherit a double portion of your spirit," Elisha replied.

"You have asked a difficult thing," Elijah said, "yet if you see me when I am taken from you, it will be yours—otherwise not."

As they were walking along and talking together, suddenly a chariot of fire and horses of fire appeared and separated the two of them, and Elijah went up to heaven in a whirlwind. Elisha saw this and cried out, "My father! My father! The chariots and horsemen of Israel!" And Elisha saw him no more. Then he took hold of his own clothes and tore them apart.

He picked up the cloak that had fallen from Elijah and went back and stood on the bank of the Jordan. (2 Kings 2:6-13)

This type of all or nothing attitude is what separates the mighty from the marginal. Fifty men hung back where it was comfortable (no extra effort required), while Elisha dogged Elijah's steps, determined to grasp the blessing! On which side of the river do you stand? Are you following after God at all costs, living up to the calling on your life and your gifts, or are you standing back, first waiting to see what He will do for you? Are you satisfied with a sample of God's blessings, or do you want the double portion? You know what this really comes down to? Loving God more than anything else and wanting what He is holding in His hands more than anything you can grasp for yourself by your own efforts. When you want supernatural blessings and abundance, you have to be willing to stretch beyond all that you hold dear or find familiar. You must be willing to do the work, go the extra mile. You must be willing to lay your entire life on the line for the prize.

> Let us fix our eyes on *Jesus,* the author and perfecter of our faith, who for the *joy* set *before him* endured the cross, scorning its shame, and sat down at the right hand of the throne of God. (Hebrews 12:2)

> Do nothing out of selfish ambition or vain conceit, but in humility consider others better than yourselves. Each of *you should look not only to your own interests, but also to the interests of others.*
>
> Your attitude should be the same as that of Christ Jesus:

> Who, being in very nature God,
>> did not consider equality with God something to be
>>> grasped,
> but made himself nothing,
>> taking the very nature of a servant,

being made in human likeness.
And being found in appearance as a man,
   he humbled himself
   and became obedient to death—even death on a cross!
Therefore God exalted him to the highest place
   and gave him the name that is above every name.
     (Philippians 2:3-9)

Contrary to the world's system, in God's kingdom the way up is down. Even Jesus had to be willing to sacrifice His very life in order to be blessed with us as His prize. Now I just heard somebody say, "We're no prize," but we are to Him. So great was His love for us that He was not willing to see any of us perish, so He made the ultimate unselfish move in order to save us and preserve us for Himself. We, like Jesus and the saints of old, must not draw back from the concept of laying our personal desires and our lives on the line to take hold of the promises of God.

They overcame him [Satan]
   by the blood of the Lamb
   and by the word of their testimony;
they did not love their lives so much
   as to shrink from *death*. (Revelation 12:11)

IN IT BUT NOT OF IT

The three Hebrew boys in the book of Daniel didn't care what anybody had to say when the king confronted them about whom they were going to worship. They were not willing to compromise themselves for earthly favor and blessing. Losing their lives meant nothing in the face of doing something that would betray the heart of the God they served. They were bold in their refusal to compromise. Though they worked for the most powerful monarch on the face of the earth at the time, they were always cognizant of whom they truly served.

> Shadrach, Meshach and Abednego replied to the king, "O Nebuchadnezzar, we do not need to defend ourselves before you in this matter. If we are thrown into the blazing furnace, the God we serve is able to save us from it, and he will rescue us from your hand, O king. But even if he does not, we want you to know, O king, that we will not serve your gods or worship the image of gold you have set up." (Daniel 3:16-18)

How could God ignore such unwavering faith?! As King Nebuchadnezzar had them thrown into the fiery furnace, the Lord Himself met them there. He walked with them through the fire. And when they were pulled out, their garments didn't even smell of smoke. God's presence in the furnace was more than an answer to the youths' bold proclamation. This special visitation would further the purposes of God and make an irrefutable impact on King Nebuchadnezzar and the nation he "ruled."

> Nebuchadnezzar then approached the opening of the blazing furnace and shouted, "Shadrach, Meshach and Abednego, servants of the Most High God, come out! Come here!"

So Shadrach, Meshach and Abednego came out of the fire, and the satraps, prefects, governors and royal advisers crowded around them. They saw that the fire had not harmed their bodies, nor was a hair of their heads singed; their robes were not scorched, and there was no smell of fire on them.

Then Nebuchadnezzar said, "Praise be to the God of Shadrach, Meshach and Abednego, who has sent his angel and rescued his servants! They trusted in him and defied the king's command and were willing to give up their lives rather than serve or worship any god except their own God. Therefore I decree that the people of any nation or language who say anything against the God of Shadrach, Meshach and Abednego be cut into pieces and their houses be turned into piles of rubble, for no other god can save in this way."

Then the king promoted Shadrach, Meshach and Abednego in the province of Babylon. (Daniel 3:26-30)

Now *that's* what I'm talking about! God was glorified by the faith of Shadrach, Meshach, and Abednego, their enemies were destroyed, and they were crowned with favor and blessed with promotions. Remember, "Whoever tries to keep his life will lose it, and whoever loses his life will preserve it" (Luke 17:33).

Are you still lost in the land of "What am I going to get out of it?" Or have you yelled the war cry "Whatever the cost, I'm willing to pay it in order to gain God's best and richest for my life"?

THE WAY TO A MAN'S HEART

Like Esther, we must have an "If I perish, I perish" attitude if we truly want to get the King's attention and see our desires fulfilled. Of course, that's a lot easier to achieve when our desires are honorable ones. Remember, your favor and blessings affect the kingdom at large.

> [Mordecai] sent back this answer [to Esther]: "Do not think that because you are in the king's house you alone of all the Jews will escape. For if you remain silent at this time, relief and deliverance for the Jews will arise from another place, but you and your father's family will perish. And who knows but that you have come to royal position for such a time as this?"
>
> Then Esther sent this reply to Mordecai: "Go, gather together all the Jews who are in Susa, and fast for me. Do not eat or drink for three days, night or day. I and my maids will fast as you do. When this is done, I will go to the king, even though it is against the law. And if I perish, I perish." (Esther 4:13-16)

You might be wondering where I'm going with this. Here's what I want you to get: Esther pressed her way into the king's court to beg for the life of others. When she finally finds herself in his presence, he is so pleased to see her that he offers her up to half of the kingdom.

But by now this girlfriend has completely gotten over herself. She stays focused on the needs of others. She invites the king to dinner, serves him, waits for him to ask her what she needs—and then she does something not many desperate women I know would do. She stifles her request and invites him to another dinner. She bides her time, allowing the king to indulge in her adoration of him before broaching the subject of her wants. Once the king has been thoroughly satisfied and is literally bursting at the seams to bless Esther with something, she submits her need to him. Not only does he give her what she has asked for, but he gives her above and beyond her wildest dreams. The king wipes out Esther's enemies, reverses their plot against her and the Jews, takes all of their property and possessions, gives them to Esther, and promotes her uncle Mordecai! Her selflessness and servant's attitude got her everything she wanted, plus some stuff she hadn't thought of.

One thing that struck me was how Esther worded her petition to the king. It speaks volumes about how far many of us have strayed in our prayer life.

> Then the king extended the gold scepter to Esther and she arose and stood before him.
>
> *"If it pleases the king,"* she said, *"and if he regards me with favor* and *thinks it the right thing to do, and if he is pleased with me,* let an order be written overruling the dispatches that Haman son of Hammedatha, the Agagite, devised and wrote to destroy the Jews in all the king's provinces." (Esther 8:4-5)

When was the last time you prayed in such a way that acknowledged the Lord's sovereign choice? I remember the old folks who used to say, "I'm going to do so and so, Lord willing." But, sadly, we've gotten past that. Now the attitude for many is that God just ought to do as we ask. Never mind if it is a bad idea. Never mind that it doesn't fit into His kingdom agenda. Never mind that we have unfinished business with Him we need to settle first. We want what we want.

But Esther submitted her desire before the king. She submitted herself to his wisdom and judgment. She yielded to how he felt about the matter. She did not assume anything. When was the last time you asked God to judge your request? Esther recognized the king had a choice in the matter, and he acted on her behalf. How could he harden his heart against one who was so humbly submitted, even to the point of death? Wow! That is truly a compelling example for us, though the bottom line is clear: When nothing else matters more to us than what pleases God, He is more than willing to extend His favor and shower us with blessings from on high.

Which brings us full circle back to Mary. Mary surrendered everything to become a willing and cheerful servant, and she was blessed.

Thoughts to Ponder

- What is your attitude toward servanthood? Do you serve God cheerfully or only when it suits your interests?
- How dear to your heart are the things that you cling to? Are you willing to surrender your life to God's decisions even if they don't coincide with yours?
- Do you give God a choice in the matter when you submit your requests to Him? What do you think He would do if you did?

- Do you understand how using your gifts and talents tie into serving God?
- What dream has He given you that you haven't pursued because of the work involved? Have you replaced God's abilities with your insecurities?

ELEVEN

no rest for the weary?

ALLOWING GOD TO PLAN HIS WORK AND WORK HIS PLAN

> Mary stayed with Elizabeth for about three months
> and then returned home.
>
> LUKE 1:56

If you are anything like me, you have probably thought, "How could Mary take a vacation at a time like this?" Didn't she wonder what Joseph was thinking? It's not as if she could call him on the phone and find out! What transpired while she was away? What kind of reception would she encounter when she returned? Would they all be waiting at the city gate to stone her to death? Shouldn't she get back home quickly and try to explain her circumstances? In spite of the thoughts that could have been swirling through her mind, Mary clung to her confidence that God was able to handle perfectly all things concerning her.

What do you do when God has promised you something so incredible that you yourself have no power to bring it to pass? What do you do when the call on your life might cause you to be misunderstood, judged, ridiculed, or resented? All you can do is *rest* in the Lord and in the power of

His might, not yours. By His Spirit the things God has promised will be accomplished. You must simply await His cues and not move before then, no matter how long the wait. "But I've got to do something, Michelle!" you say, though you don't know just what. After all, what do you do when there's *nothing else* you can *do?* The answer comes back from God: rest. "But...but...," you say. There, there, I do understand!

And I also know that we live in a society that doesn't allow rest because our worth is determined by what we *do.* However, God does not call us to *do* anything; He calls us to *be.* Being is far more difficult for most of us. "So what do I do while I am simply *being?*" you might be wondering. Well, God has several suggestions.

> Now then, *stand still* and see this great thing the LORD is about to do before your eyes! (1 Samuel 12:16)

> You will not have to fight this battle. Take up your positions; *stand* firm and see the deliverance the LORD will give you.... Do not be afraid; do not be discouraged. (2 Chronicles 20:17)

> Some *trust* in chariots and some in horses,
>   but we *trust* in the name of the LORD our God.
>   (Psalm 20:7)

> *Be still,* and *know* that I am God;
>   I will *be* exalted among the nations,
>   I will *be* exalted in the earth. (Psalm 46:10)

This is what the Sovereign LORD, the Holy One of
Israel, says:

"In repentance and rest is your salvation,
   in quietness and *trust* is your strength,
   but you would have none of it." (Isaiah 30:15)

Trust in the LORD and do good;
   dwell in the land and enjoy safe pasture.
Delight yourself in the LORD
   and he will give you the desires of your heart.
Commit your way to the LORD;
   trust in him and he will do this:
He will make your righteousness shine like the dawn,
   the justice of your cause like the noonday sun.
Be still before the LORD and wait patiently for him.
   (Psalm 37:3-7)

See? There's plenty for you to do. Be still, stand firm, trust God, delight
yourself in the Lord, commit your way to Him, and wait patiently for Him
to do His thing.

TAKE FIVE

For musicians, a rest is a beautiful thing. It is the pause that affords them
the opportunity to catch their breath and continue the melody or to shift

tempos and create new moods in the piece they are playing. For athletes, rest is crucial. It is a time of restoration and rebuilding of strength in preparation for the next round. Their rest is necessary for victory. For a farmer, giving the fields rest makes the difference between good crops and mediocre ones, life and death.

> When a farmer plows for planting, does he plow
> continually?
> Does he keep on breaking up and harrowing the soil?
> (Isaiah 28:24)

> Be patient, then, brothers, until the Lord's coming. See how the *farmer* waits for the land to yield its valuable crop and how patient he is for the autumn and spring rains. (James 5:7)

> For six years you are to sow your fields and harvest the crops, but during the seventh year let the land lie unplowed and unused. Then the poor among your people may get food from it, and the wild animals may eat what they leave. Do the same with your vineyard and your olive grove.
> Six days do your work, but on the seventh day do not work, so that your ox and your donkey may rest and the slave born in your household, and the alien as well, may be refreshed. (Exodus 23:10-12)

> But in the seventh year the *land* is to have a sabbath of
> *rest,* a sabbath to the LORD. Do not sow your fields or
> prune your vineyards. (Leviticus 25:4)

Why is rest so vital to the land and the seed? Because if you relentlessly turn the soil, the rich nutrients embedded deep within it become exposed to and depleted by the elements. Also to keep planting continually in the same field sucks the life out of the earth. The crops are not as lush, sweet, or nutritious. God knew that even the land needs to regain its strength in order to yield good fruit. For all things, there is serious merit in rest.

Even God rested. Does that mean He was inactive? I don't believe so. I picture him sitting back and allowing everything He had put in place to settle into the divine order He had ordained. I imagine Him taking a deep breath and, as He exhales, seeing that breath give the finishing life-giving touches to all His creation.

What you must know in order to really rest is that while you are resting, God is still busy on your behalf. Esther retired for the night after her first banquet with the king, but he was unable to sleep. God troubled him in the night in order to make it clear to him who was truly on his side in the kingdom. This episode set the king up to show favor to Esther the next day when she appealed to him for the lives of her family and her people.

Similarly, when Ruth informed Boaz that she was in need of a redeemer and then returned home, Naomi told her to simply bide her time. Boaz would not rest until the matter was settled. Sure enough, Boaz headed straight for the city gate to negotiate with the next of kin in line for Ruth's hand. In the end Ruth was blessed with not only a wealthy and loving husband, but also with a place in the lineage of Christ.

As I write this I chuckle. I am watching with trepidation the 2000 presidential returns. It is a close race, and I am concerned about the candidates' platforms. So why the chuckle? It never fails—the minute you learn a principle, you will be tested on it. By now I should know the drill. I have to stop and remind myself that regardless of who wins, the just will live by faith, the simple faith that God is in control. Ultimately, only one truly sits on the throne and commands the affairs of men and women alike.

The bottom line: Even when we don't see anything with our natural eye, God is still at work.

> He also said, "This is what the kingdom of God is like. A man scatters seed on the ground. Night and day, whether he sleeps or gets up, the seed sprouts and grows, though he does not know how. All by itself the soil produces grain—first the stalk, then the head, then the full kernel in the head. As soon as the grain is ripe, he puts the sickle to it, because the harvest has come." (Mark 4:26-29)

> However, as it is written:

> "No *eye* has *seen*,
>   no ear has heard,
> no mind has conceived
>   what God has prepared for those who love him."
>   (1 Corinthians 2:9)

While some trust in the arm of flesh, those who believe must trust the Spirit of God to bring the seed of our dreams and our faith to life.

> Let the beloved of the LORD *rest* secure in him,
>> for he shields him all day long,
>> and the one the LORD loves rests between his
>> shoulders. (Deuteronomy 33:12)

In other words, don't fret! God's got it! God's got *you!* Your desires and longings are safe and secure in the breast of God. *How should I rest?* you might be wondering. Here's the answer that may make you quake: Simply take a deep breath and let go. Chances are that the things God has promised you are so huge and overwhelming there is absolutely nothing you can do to bring them to pass. You have no choice but to continue on right where you are, with nothing more than the expectation of things to come from God.

GIVE IT A REST

As Abraham set out for a land he knew nothing of, and though he was walking, he rested in the promise that God would prosper him and bring him to a place that was greater than where he had been. However, when it came to the matter of fatherhood, Abraham struggled. Why? Because he was distracted by his own flesh and his own abilities. Anytime we stop to evaluate our own abilities, we will be unable to rest. There is little we can truly accomplish in our own strength. In the long run it is far easier to admit this than to spend our energy proving it to ourselves! When we attempt to "help" God carry out His plans and refuse to rest in His ways and His timing, we make drastic mistakes that can have far-reaching consequences.

The irony in all of this is that God is not moved by our self-centered efforts. He merely waits until we have exhausted ourselves. When we finally throw our hands up in dismay, He says, "Good, you are finally out of the way."

Rest must use faith as a pillow. When we lay down our own efforts and stop trying to make things happen, then we sink into our pillow of faith, safe and secure in His abilities, and allow God to take up our part. In our weakness He reveals His strength. He longs to have the elbowroom to perform the miraculous in our lives. The reason we struggle so with the issue of rest is because it makes us feel helpless. To rest is to place yourself at the mercy of God.

I recently experienced this in a dramatic way. If you have read my other books, you are aware of this part of my testimony. One day as I was walking across the street, a man driving a delivery van stepped on the gas as I stepped in front of his vehicle. To make a long story short, I suffered a severe injury to my knee. A major tendon was completely severed. Five years later, after I had three operations, underwent the trial of literally learning to walk again, and spent a year-and-a-half more in bed than out of it, my lawsuit saw the inside of a courtroom. It was a trial made for television. The defense was ruthless because they had no defense. The driver admitted his negligence and guilt. My doctor and therapist testified to the seriousness of my injury. My employer confirmed my inability to work. After attempting to cause a mistrial, the defense attacked me and distracted the jury from my permanently damaged knee by concentrating on my lifestyle.

They sneered as they told the panel that I had gained an extraordinary life as the result of my accident.

They pointed to the fact that I had completed my first book while I was lying in bed and, as a result, had secured a new career for myself. They told these men and women that I now led the glamorous life of an author who had penned nine more books in three years, flown around the country speaking, and co-hosted a television show. Since I had done so well for myself, they concluded, I should not be compensated because I had not really suffered at all. I sat there thinking of the excruciating pain I had endured after each surgery and throughout my rehabilitation—of how, despite my new life, I struggled with a leg that would never be the same again. I thought of the pain I still experience and how it now takes double the effort to do what I could easily do before the accident. I thought of my therapist telling me, "Because of the trauma associated with your injury, your leg will never have the strength it had before." I felt helpless as my attorney said the words "We rest our case." I was now at the mercy of the jury.

As we waited for the verdict, the defense offered a settlement that was unacceptable to my attorney. By her calculations the worst I would get from the jury would be equal to what they offered. I sought the counsel of others and they agreed. And so we waited. Finally we were summoned back to the court. The jury had been swayed to be hostile. Though they acknowledged that the driver was guilty of hitting me and compensated me for my medical fees, they did not feel that I should be awarded anything substantial for my pain and suffering. In the end they awarded me less than the insurance had offered to settle for. The judge was mortified, as was the man who had hit me. My attorney was stunned, and even the defense team was surprised. To be perfectly honest, I stood there trying to find God and get an explanation. How do you rest at a time like this? How do you continue to feel blessed and highly favored when things aren't going the way you think they should?

How would I express to my attorney my faith in God's goodness after an outcome like that? What would I say to the man who had hit me? As I listened to his heartfelt apology, I told him I had never held him responsible for my pain and asked him if he believed in God. Yes, he said, he did. I asked him if he knew the story of Joseph. He said he had read it in the Koran. He was Muslim. I told him I felt the words of Joseph were apropos to my situation. What was meant for evil had been turned around for my good. It was true. I had sustained an injury with lasting consequences. But during that time of rest and healing I had stepped into the center of God's will for my life. I had never been still enough prior to the accident to complete what He had called me to do, but adverse circumstances brought me to a place of yielding. Now I'm living the life of my dreams. It was true: I had gained an extraordinarily blessed life because of this trial.

THE KINDNESS OF STRANGERS

Perhaps the lesson for me that day was never to place my confidence in man but always to rely on God. Indeed He had taken care of me and even prospered me during my convalescence. I thought back to the time of my accident. Two weeks before it occurred, I had acquired a freelance contract on a retainer basis. I was to be paid a certain amount every month whether or not I worked. God, in His omnipotent foresight, had looked down the road, anticipated my need, and secured my provision for this difficult time. With a grateful heart I was able to count my blessings that had not decreased during that time but had increased instead. It was a miracle, so *totally* a God thing that I could not have planned it better myself!

The Lord had proven to me that I could rest in Him for not only what I required but also for what I desired—*and above and beyond!* As I shared this with the driver who had hit me, he gazed at me in amazement. I continued, "Hey, there are people out there who don't have a leg. I'm happy to be limping. It could be worse." He could not understand why I was not bitter. I had to chuckle at the irony of the whole situation. The defense was right: I was so blessed that I didn't need men to bless me! My God was completely able, all by Himself, to arrange for me to receive anything I needed. Who knows why things turned out the way they did? Perhaps this man's salvation was at stake. But since God doesn't waste anyone's life or time, I think the end of the story is yet to be revealed.

I remember the Israelites, who were afraid to allow the land to rest every seven years in accordance with God's command. Four hundred and ninety years later, as they headed to Babylon, God tallied up their years of disobedience and determined that they must spend seventy years in captivity in order for the land to have the full rest it was due. God will get you to rest one way or the other. And it's all for your own good. A failure to rest leads us into the bondage of self-effort, which usually yields only deep hurt and disappointment. Whether you war for the blessing of getting married, starting a ministry, obtaining a dream, succeeding in your career, attaining financial success—whatever it is that you are trying to accomplish in your own strength—it's time to stop and rest in order to be blessed.

> There remains, then, a Sabbath-rest for the people of
> God; for anyone who enters God's rest also rests from

his own work, just as God did from his. (Hebrews 4:9-10)

As we cease our labors and wait for God to make His entrance, we must believe His promises no matter what we see or hear. Sometimes His promises seem too incredible to believe, and we stumble over them in pursuit of our own goals and dreams. We can't stand the suspense!

When the Lord commanded Israel to allow the land to rest, He also reassured the people that they shouldn't worry about what they were going to eat. He promised them that He would make the land produce enough food to cover the year that they didn't plant and the year of sowing and reaping. But that was just too hard for the Israelites to believe. What if God didn't keep His promise and they starved? No, no, no, they had better take matters into their own hands and keep right on planting. And so in the end they didn't get to plant anything for seventy years. At least not in Israel. Despite all of their doubt and disobedience, the Lord urged them to get back on track.

> *This* is what the LORD says:
>
> "Stand at the crossroads and look;
>   ask for the ancient paths,
> ask where the good *way* is, and *walk* in it,
>   and you will find rest for your souls."
>   (Jeremiah 6:16)

At every step along the way, God will always require us to take a season of rest before moving to the next level. Take the time to remember His first word to you. Regain your strength, rearrange your priorities, and get further instructions for the next phase. You will never be able to move forward without the Word of God, without the prompting of the Holy Spirit saying, "Go this way, I'm right behind you." Otherwise you will end up under a broom tree like Elijah, running from the threats of the enemy, too spent and tired to remember God's promises (1 Kings 19).

Mary did not forget. She took God's promise and ran with it. She did her part and left the balance to God. He took care of the seemingly impossible. This young woman accepted God's Word and rested in the knowledge that what He had said He was able to perform, regardless of what anyone might say or do. He would take care of His own and guard His promises jealously; therefore, no harm would come to her. She would see the fulfillment of His plan birthed in her own life. She felt safe and secure under His watchful eye. Mary rested, and she was blessed.

Thoughts to Ponder

- Do you trust God to carry out His promises in your life?
- Do you feel the need to help Him bring His word to pass? When things aren't going the way you imagined they would, do you doubt His word to you?
- Do you question God's goodness? Or do you trust the way He takes you?
- Do you leave God options for your life?
- Do you feel paralyzed by rest? Why? Do you believe that God is still working long after you have stopped striving?
- How can you refresh yourself while you wait on Him?

living with open hands

MASTERING HOW TO CATCH THE RAIN

"I am the Lord's servant," Mary answered. "May it
be to me as you have said."

LUKE 1:38

Can we talk about the blessedness of being completely open to whatever
God wants to do with you? That is an incredible place to be. I remember
when I first came to the Lord. I decided that I didn't want to be one of
those "weird" Christians. I understood that we were a peculiar people, but
I didn't want to be strange. However, I was in quite a dilemma. One part of
me wanted to be whatever God wanted me to be, but another part of me
was afraid to find out what that would be. I didn't want to end up on some
television show with over-the-top hair and outrageous makeup looking
ridiculously sanctified. I wanted to be cool and saved at the same time.
Somehow I didn't see those two things merging. I was at war within.

Whenever I felt myself being stretched, I was quick to clamp down
and short-circuit my growth. I didn't want to know more. I wanted to stay
the same. So stay the same I did—until I got good and bored with being
stagnant. I tell you, sometimes when God says, "Okay," it's *not* a good

thing. A good friend of mine once told me, "Until the pain of staying the same is greater than the pain of change, you won't change." When God said "okay" to my desire to not change, I got so sick of me I was ready for whatever He wanted to do. Then I was pleasantly surprised to find that I liked the things He had in mind. But I must admit that I remained suspicious for quite a while, thinking He was buttering me up with all the things He knew I liked before He pulled a fast one on me. I kept glancing at the mirror out the corner of my eye to see if He was rearranging my hair.

But the longer I walked with God, the more I came to realize that He had fabulous taste and incredible ideas. Every time I surrendered to Him and allowed Him to do His thing in my life, I ended up saying, "Wow! I couldn't have come up with that in a million years!" I found out that the happiest place to be was in the center of His perfect will. The doors and opportunities that were opened to me were in accordance with His kingdom plan, but my joy was the icing on the cake. What a powerful combination: His will, my fulfillment.

I DID IT MY WAY

So many miss the potential for blessings by clinging to their own ideas, goals, and desires. They bang their heads against the wall over and over again and come to the conclusion that God is cruel. As I wrote in my devotional *His Love Always Finds Me,* "In straining to hear You, my questions drown out Your answers and I accuse You of not listening. In grasping to receive Your blessing, my hands get in the way and I drop Your promises." Meanwhile God sits pointing to the yield sign and the detour up ahead that leads to a better way.

God loves us so much that He presses past our outer countenance; He looks in our heart and sees that our desire is really what He wants. He gently nudges us into the right spot by allowing failure and the passage of time to bring us to our knees at the place where He waits, ready and willing to meet us and guide us back onto the right track.

> Whether you turn to the right or to the left, your ears will hear a voice behind you, saying, "*This* is the *way; walk* in it." (Isaiah 30:21)

> In his heart a *man plans* his course,
>   but the LORD determines his steps. (Proverbs 16:9)

> Many are the *plans* in a *man's* heart,
>   but it is the LORD's purpose that prevails.
>   (Proverbs 19:21)

GOD'S SIGHT IS FORESIGHT

Thank God His purposes prevail! When I was in college, I fell in love with a very handsome young man. He was my sun, my moon, my everything. But neither of my fathers, Mr. Hammond or Mr. McKinney, could stand him. They prevailed upon my mother to get me to end the relationship. Well, talk about a modern-day *Romeo and Juliet!* My, my, my—the drama of it all. The tears, the pleadings, the clandestine meetings, the railings at the unfairness of life, and the cruelty of my parents. I concluded that they had never been in love and therefore would never understand that life just wasn't worth living if I couldn't see the light of my life. Finally I was shipped off to another college in another city. Time and distance did what my parents could not, and eventually his golden halo melted into an ordinary Afro.

Seven years later this man resurfaced, still professing his love for me at a time when I was open and vulnerable. He expressed the desire to see me and talk about getting back together. By then, however, I had become a Christian. The Lord warned me to flee his advances, and though I didn't understand why at the time, I'm glad I did. Years passed, and his life went from bad to worse, to the type of life I would not have wanted to share. About a week ago I learned he had murdered an eighty-year-old man by bludgeoning him to death with a two-by-four. What a shock! I could not picture this man doing such a thing. Who knew he had such a violent temper—and whether I would have been a victim of it? God did. God, in His infinite mercy, shielded me from danger even when I did not know Him. May His name be praised! What if I had insisted on my own way? Where would I be today? The thought is not one I care to consider.

TO BE OR NOT TO BE

I believe that as we walk before God with open hands and allow Him to take and give as He pleases, we will walk between the raindrops more often than not. For every time that I have failed to yield to His still, small, and gentle voice, I've regretted it. Every time I please myself first, I end up not so pleased at all. Although God delights in us coming to Him as children, He also exhorts us to grow up, to be perfect—not in the sense of perfectionism, but in the sense of being mature.

When I was a *child,* I talked like a *child,* I thought like a *child,* I reasoned like a *child. When* I became a man, I put childish ways behind me. (1 Corinthians 13:11)

Be perfect, therefore, as your heavenly Father is perfect. (Matthew 5:48)

Is it a Catch-22 situation? While Jesus tells us we must be like children, He also tells us to grow up. *Well, which one is it, Jesus?* It's important to understand that in the first case He was discussing our belief system. A little child believes anything adults say, and God is delighted when we have *childlike faith* in what He says. However, *childish behavior* is characterized by selfishness, petulance, wanting to have one's own way, not accepting correction willingly, and throwing manipulative tantrums. In contrast, maturity teaches us to be open to correction, change, and options, to be both flexible and generous.

Brothers, stop thinking like children. In regard to evil *be* infants, but in your thinking *be* adults. (1 Corinthians 14:20)

Jesus answered, "If you want to *be perfect,* go, sell your possessions and give to the poor, and you will have treasure in heaven. Then come, follow me." (Matthew 19:21)

Maturity teaches us that God's pleasure becomes our pleasure. His pleasure is to use you; in return you will be blessed. I think of Mary saying, "Yes,

Lord, completely yes," harboring no agenda of her own. Hers would be a lifelong call, first as a woman of God, then as a mother, then as a wife.

As a mother, Mary would have to be willing to surrender her child to the world and watch Him die. Mothers have a difficult time releasing their children, and yet Mary walked with the understanding that although Jesus was her son, truly He was not. She was merely the vessel chosen to raise Him and give Him back to God. And, actually, that is all any parent is called to do.

I believe the prophecy of future pain that Mary received in the temple applies to every parent. A sword pierces the hearts of parents several times throughout life as they watch their charges go through the difficult passage from infant to adult. Even so, they must release their children into the hands of God and dare to believe that He is able to keep that which is committed to Him. I know that it is difficult to believe, but He loves your children more than is humanly possible—more than even you do! And He longs for their victory far above your greatest longing. I believe that on the day Mary encouraged Jesus to perform His first miracle, she watched Him with a divided heart. Part of her was proud of what He had become; the other part knew it was time to cut the apron strings.

HOTEL, MOTEL, HOLIDAY INN

Besides yielding to God in her parenting, Mary the wife yielded to her husband's correction. I find it interesting that prior to Mary's marriage, the angel spoke first with her and then with Joseph. After she became his wife, however, all angelic instructions were given to Joseph. Mary submitted to him as unto the Lord. This was a good thing, a life-saving thing. Can you imagine what would have happened if she hadn't submitted?

You'll recall that shortly after Jesus was born, Herod decreed all new-borns up to the age of two be killed, so fearful was he that a king had been born to replace him. The angel told Joseph to take Mary and flee to Egypt. What if she had put her hand on her hip and said, "I'm not going any-where. God didn't tell me that. He talks to me, too, you know. I want to go home and show my baby to my family and friends, thank you." The out-come would have been quite different, to say the least. Mary's obedience meant a blessing to them all.

Living life with open hands demands that we be prepared for sudden changes. Sometimes God wants to change the route of our lives for our own protection and for increased blessings. Think of Mary and Joseph as they traveled to Bethlehem and, after an especially wearing day, finding no room at the inn. I've got to pause here and consider my own irritation when I arrive at a hotel after traveling all day, only to find that my reserva-tion has been lost somewhere in the computer. I have to take a deep breath and exercise self-control when I would rather fuss and ask, "What *is* the problem? You knew I was coming. Why don't you have your act together? Can't you see that I'm exhausted? *Where* is the manager?!"

Taking the temperature of our impatient microwave generation, I imag-ine the Mary of today saying, "Look, don't you know I'm carrying the Son of God? I'm a VIP! I think you'd better look again and find me a room *some-where* in this joint 'cause I'm not taking no for an answer." But the real Mary settled gratefully and gracefully into a stable for the night. Mary did not view her circumstances as a reason for preferential treatment. She con-tinued in humility, simply considering it an honor to be of service to her Lord. She chose to make the best out of an undesirable situation. Perhaps there was a good reason for her not to stay at the inn. We will never know in this life. But Mary certainly didn't learn any lessons the hard way that night.

But, unlike Mary, when we decide how things should go and how we should be treated, we get in trouble. We will always think that we are due something more than what we have received, and from time to time, that expectation becomes a stumbling block to our spiritual and natural growth. So many people in ministry today fall prey to the devices of the enemy, who whispers the same thoughts that once assaulted his own mind and cost him his heavenly post. They begin to think that they are worthy of praise, honor, and special treatment. This way of thinking leads them to exercise liberties that cause them to fall. No matter how coveted a position we find ourselves in, we must continue to see ourselves as servants of the Most High God, accepting each accolade with the utmost of humility, offering the praise back to Him who truly deserves it. After all, it is not by our own works that we achieve anything lest we find occasion to boast. It is totally by the grace of God that we find ourselves where we are. If this is our attitude, we, like Mary, will gracefully accept every situation we find ourselves in, trusting God and His purposes to triumph on every occasion.

WHERE HE LEADS ME...

As we look down the Hall of Biblical Fame in search of inspiring characters who were blessed above measure, one thing rings true: These people opened their hands to God. People like Abraham. Truly Abraham was open. He had to be. He had no idea where he was going! But God knew. I will be the first to admit it: I hate change—hate it, hate it, hate it! And doesn't it seem as if the minute you settle into a groove and get comfortable, God comes along and says, "Okay, it's time to pull up the stakes and move on"?

"But wait a minute, God!" you say. "I was just getting comfortable."

God knows that "comfortable" is a dangerous place. The more comfortable we become, the less dependent on God we become. And so He shakes up the mix of our lives and keeps us moving. When we arrive at the destination He has selected, we rejoice. "Gee, Lord!" we exclaim, "You should have told me—I would have done this sooner." Well, that's exactly why He didn't. You would have moved ahead of His plan and missed it. God wants us to be open to His voice and His leading every step of the way. He will always lead us down the right path.

> The LORD is my shepherd, I shall not be in want.
>> He makes me lie down in green pastures,
> he leads me beside quiet waters,
>> he restores my soul.
> He guides me in paths of righteousness
>> for his name's sake....
> You anoint my head with oil;
>> my cup overflows.
> Surely goodness and love will follow me
>> all the days of my life,
> and I will dwell in the house of the LORD
>> forever. (Psalm 23:1-3,5-6)

> All these *blessings* will come upon you and accompany you if you obey the LORD your God. (Deuteronomy 28:2)

Sheep are devout followers of the shepherd. They are totally dependent, obedient, and trusting. Where he leads, they follow. The few who are inattentive and misguided wander off and are devoured by wolves or fall off cliffs. But those who follow the shepherd's path are led to the best areas of pasture and the clearest brooks; they spend their days in peace. These are the blessings that are so taken for granted. Yet provision and peace are lacking in the lives of many who stray from His path. They have provided for themselves but have no peace. Some have peace but struggle with provision. The Good Shepherd offers both.

The Shepherd's path leads to blessings, unlimited provision, and rest. But that's just half of it. Do you know what it is like to be followed by goodness? To have blessings chasing after you? This is a phenomenal thought. Many feel they have to run after a good blessing, but no—God said His blessings would run after you if you follow Him! I like the sound of that.

LIVING THE GOOD LIFE

Have you ever known someone who just seems to lead a serendipitous life? Good things just come their way. Their conversation always goes something like this: "I was walking down the street minding my own business, and I happened to run into so-and-so. We were standing there talking when I happened to mention this and that, and so-and-so said, 'I just met someone who could help you with that.' We ended up stopping off to have a cup of coffee and discuss it further. We were sitting there when this *very* person walked in—can you believe it? So my friend mentioned my need, and this person told me he was just thinking that someone needed to do what I wanted to do. And *just* like that he told me he would give me everything I needed to make it happen! *Just like that!*"

Meanwhile, you're standing there saying to yourself, *How does this sort of thing happen to this person all the time?* I'll tell you how: Such people are open to the possibilities God sets before them. They embrace the possibilities and run with them, but not too fast. They don't want to miss God's next turn. As they go, the pieces of their lives fall into place because they have stronger belief in the power of God than in their own ingenuity. They are fully cognizant of the fact that they, in and of themselves, don't make anything happen. They wake up in the morning ready to go with the flow. They are open to the moment. They live in the moment. They are not myopic. They are open to change. They are ready to go wherever the Spirit of the Lord takes them that day. (The result of this attitude toward life holds true for unbelievers as well as believers. Unbelievers just give credit to forces such as luck, a higher power, or whatever suits their fancy. But those who come to know the Lord look back in hindsight and acknowledge that God was wooing them to His side as He sprinkled blessings along the path leading them to His throne.)

Getting back to Abraham: He was willing to sacrifice his only son, Isaac. He was willing to give up the child of promise if that was what God wanted. Of course, God stopped him and provided a ram in a thicket for the sacrifice, but the test revealed where Abraham's heart was. Where is your heart? Do you just want what you want? Do you fail to ask God what He thinks about it because you fear He'll tell you it's a bad idea? Oh yeah, we go to the land of I Want from time to time, but we need to leave that country *real* fast. There are giants in that land who will have you for dinner. In God-First country, however, there is great safety and blessing. Because Abraham's heart matched the heart of God the Father (who was also willing to sacrifice His Son for our sakes), Abraham was made the father of many nations. He could be trusted with blessings because he did not rejoice in the gift more than the Giver. And that is what being blessed really boils down to.

> For where your *treasure* is, there your *heart* will be also.
> (Matthew 6:21)

Is your heart wrapped around the blessings or wrapped up in the Blesser? You've got to have your priorities straight. God will not give you anything that will distract you from Him. And when we grasp things for ourselves, they might come into our hands, but they may not remain there for long. And when they come by self-propelled means and do remain, the inevitable pain that results doesn't make the prize worthwhile. Anything that does not come in accordance with God's timing or purpose brings hard lessons with it. Trust me, every good thing is not a blessing if you're not ready to receive it. It's like putting a two-year-old child behind the wheel of a Porsche and allowing him to drive. Both would be destroyed. This is why God would like us to release to Him both the timing and the manner in which we will be blessed. He chooses well, my friend. Allow Him to select your presents.

TAKING GOD OUT OF THE BOX

God has never given me a blessing I didn't like. I went to New York one year to visit a friend and buy a ring for myself in celebration of my birthday. My friend and I went from store to store looking at different baubles. She was quite a connoisseur of jewelry, diamonds in particular, and found something wrong with everything I selected. After a long day, I returned home bone weary and disappointed that I had nothing on my finger.

Later, after dinner, we were going through some photo albums of hers when I spotted a ring in one of the pictures that made me exclaim. On that note she jumped up and said, "Oh, now you've ruined my surprise." She disappeared for a moment and returned bearing a small silver platter with a little velvet box on it. She presented it to me, saying, "While we were out today, the Lord told me to give you this." My jaw dropped as I opened the box. It was that very ring I had admired in the photograph, far more beautiful than anything I had seen that day. I burst into tears, overwhelmed by the generosity of my friend, but even more so at the attentiveness of God. He knew all along what I would like and had chosen to *give it* to me. I often wondered what would have happened if I had insisted on buying one of the other rings. I think I would have missed out on a rich blessing: experiencing God's love for me and witnessing the depth of my friend's affection. Both were humbling.

Oh, if only we would close our eyes and open our hands! Did you ever play that game as a child? You never could be certain what your friends would put into your hands. Would it be a marble? A piece of candy? A leaf? A worm? Ew! This uncertainty will always remain when we are dealing with human beings, but we can always count on our heavenly Father to deliver incredible gifts.

> Which of you, if his son asks for bread, will give him
> a stone? Or if he asks for a fish, will give him a snake?
> If you, then, though you are evil, know how to give
> good gifts to your children, how much more will your

Father in heaven give good gifts to those who ask him!
(Matthew 7:9-11)

Every *good* and *perfect gift* is from above, coming down
from the Father of the heavenly lights, who does not
change like shifting shadows. (James 1:17)

God is not moody, loving us one day and raging against us the next. He
does not change His good intentions toward us. Daily He extends new
mercies and looks for our open hands, into which He wants to deposit
invaluable, immeasurable blessings. He is always faithful to deliver on His
promises.

We tend to be suspicious of God because we see Him through the haze
of what our own hearts are capable of. *We* change our minds. *We* feel stingy
or generous on any given day depending on how others treat us. *We* are
reserved with others based on past hurts and disappointments. But His
ways are not our ways; His thoughts are not our thoughts. God keeps short
accounts. He does not superimpose the past over the future. He is able to
let bygones be bygones. So no matter what you have done, He is ready to
start anew. He's ready to start blessing you all over again. Don't you just
love that about Him?

THE SECRET RECIPE FOR BLESSING

As our conversation draws to a close, let's review the pictures of reality we've
covered. Surely the pages of biblical history are clear: Those people who

were blessed the most were broken the most; they sacrificed the most. They opened their lives to God so that He could shape and mold them in preparation for the blessings to come. What are you willing to let drop from your outstretched hands? Your heart? Your life? The thing dearest to you? Everything? Can you be like Hannah, who gave the very son she longed for back to God and then received many children in return? Can you be like the mother of Moses, who placed him in a basket and set him afloat in the Nile, trusting that God would keep him? She received him back as a mighty leader. Can you be like David, who refused to seize the throne of Israel himself and instead left the timing of his coronation completely up to God? He refused to kill the very enemy who hunted him day and night for years! As evil as King Saul was, and as justified as David would have been in killing him while he had the opportunity, David released Saul to be dealt with by God.

> Abishai said to David, "Today God has delivered your enemy into your hands. Now let me pin him to the ground with one thrust of my spear; I won't strike him twice."
>
> But David said to Abishai, "Don't destroy him! Who can lay a hand on the LORD's anointed and be guiltless? As surely as the LORD lives," he said, "the LORD himself will strike him; either his time will come and he will die, or he will go into battle and perish. But the LORD forbid that I should lay a hand on the LORD's anointed. Now get the spear and water jug that are near his head, and let's go." (1 Samuel 26:8-11)

The list continues: Three Hebrew boys willingly walked into the fiery furnace and came out promoted. Jesus, the author and finisher of our faith, was insulted, bruised, broken, and crucified before He was exalted. He not only opened His hands, He opened His arms, His life, His everything. When He could have defended Himself, He did not; instead He went as a lamb to the slaughter, not saying a word.

Are we there yet? Are we willing to be in communion with Christ's suffering so that we may be blessed to reign with Him? Are you willing to be broken, given away, and blessed in order to acquire something greater? Some days I say yes. Thank God I'm saying it more often than I used to.

COME OUT WITH YOUR HANDS UP

When we sing the words to that old song, "I'm Yours, Lord, everything I am, everything I've got. I'm Yours, Lord, try me now and see. See if I can be completely Yours," we must be careful. Do we really live what we sing? "I surrender all. All to Thee, my blessed Savior, I surrender all." Do we really? If we were to tally the number of times we say no to God versus the number of times we say yes, which would be greater? Surrender yourself. Get your hands in the air, up and open in demonstration that you are neither hiding nor holding anything. What is in your hands at this very moment? Will it hinder you from getting what you truly want from the Lord?

A certain Hollywood screenwriter is said to have written many scripts, but no one ever liked any of them. After suffering from deep disillusionment, this man left California and went to live in a small town. He started noticing the incredible racial harmony of the people who lived there. He began to ask questions and was told that the harmony was the result of certain things that had transpired in the lives of the local high-school football team and the impact it had on the community. He went in search of the coaches and other involved parties and began conducting interviews. He then wrote the story and headed back to Hollywood. No one wanted to buy the rights to the story or give him the money to develop it. So he wrote the screenplay himself. He sent it out to everyone he could think of; no one wanted it. Once again he threw his hands up in the air and retreated. About that time he received a call. A powerful producer wanted to do a football film. The rest is now history. *Remember the Titans* opened to much acclaim.

The moral of the story? Your hopes might not pan out the way you want them to; *they could turn out to be even better.* Once you let go, that is. As a child, I wanted to be a rock star when I grew up—a combination of Diana Ross and Barbra Streisand. Can you imagine that? I sang my way through high school, beauty pageants, plays, and home-grown bands. I prepared myself for stardom, but it never happened. Oh, I got glimpses of it, but it never happened. I came close, but not quite. I had all the right connections and entrées. I even got a music publishing deal with a major music publishing company, but I never held that brass ring.

Instead I ended up in the world of advertising. Ironically, I got to do all the things I wanted to do and enjoyed much more financial stability. I ended up writing and producing jingles and singing them myself! I created television commercials, produced them, and met and worked with a myriad of stars. I had tickets to every event they had tickets to. The Grammys, the Oscars—you name it, I went. So what was I missing? Absolutely nothing, and I was probably staying out of a heap of trouble to boot. In retrospect I now see that that type of life would not have made me happy. Why? Because I would have ignored the greater call on my life to be a writer.

I would not have discovered this precious gift that gives me so much joy while it hopefully blesses others.

I had started my life off one way, but it ended up completely different than I thought it would, and I'm loving every minute of it. I studied to be an art director but ended up writing. I started off writing commercials and ended up writing books. I started off writing books and ended up speaking all over the place. I started off speaking and ended up singing as well! I even got the television show thrown in!

Are you getting this? Do you see how God brought me full circle? When life refused to work the way I wanted it to, I surrendered all that I held dear and decided to put one foot in front of the other, use the resources presently available to me, and go where He led. He led me to the very center and fulfillment of my dreams. He got what He wanted out of me and then added what I wanted as well. I didn't get the leftovers; I got the mother lode! I feel so blessed every day that I am alive. I feel the umbrella of His favor over me even in the moments of my life that try my faith. I know that He is faithful and that each trial that comes my way is just a test. It, too, shall pass, because I am determined to pass the test and get to the good part of kingdom living. I know what I have been called to do for Christ. I count it such a privilege to be able to utilize all of my gifts to bless others. To live and work for God is the ultimate blessing, no matter what your profession or walk of life.

TAKING OFF THE LIMITS

God is limitless. This is a resounding fact. However, for a myriad of reasons, sometimes we unintentionally limit ourselves, as well as His ability to work in our lives. It is within our power, via our choices, to cast off the limits and give God free reign in our lives. If God is limitless, we can be too. I have learned that He is not obligated to bless you in the way that you think you should be blessed, but He is motivated to bless you as much as you allow Him to. Mary the mother of Jesus knew that. As a single woman I am blessed by the fact that when Mary received this awesome call from the Lord she was a single woman. She was betrothed to Joseph, but their vows had not been consummated yet. She belonged completely to God. She was totally *available* to God. He was her focus and her center. Whither God went, she went also. Nothing stood between them. She didn't have to check with anyone else. The affairs of her life were between her and God. And so it was that she was the chosen one. Because of Mary, we have all been blessed. Now, because of her Son, Jesus, we can all qualify to be blessed and highly favored. Because of God's love for mankind we are *all* called to bear Christ to the world!

If Mary were to be the feature of a special biography program today, I believe the reporter would introduce her with something like this: "Today we would like to take a look at the life of the only person in the Bible greeted with the impressive salutation 'blessed *and* highly favored.' As we consider her life, several things will become evident about this extraordinary woman. She lived a life of purity and had an incredible relationship with God. She was extremely sensitive spiritually and possessed remarkable faith. The fruit of her life was as obvious to others as her refusal to compromise on ungodly issues. Her reputation was as flawless as her sense of discretion. This was a woman who did not insist on her own way. Instead, she was at peace with God's decisions for her life. She was open and completely available to go wherever the Spirit of God led her. Truly she was favored. Truly she was blessed. She herself uttered the very words that would be repeated throughout the ages when others referred to her: 'From now on all generations will call me blessed' (Luke 1:48)."

Thoughts to Ponder

- Do you consider yourself completely available for God to use as He pleases?
- What areas in your life do you still reserve for yourself?
- What do you think God would do with your life if you let Him have his way completely?
- Should He come calling with some amazing assignment for your life, are you ready? Are your hands open? Are you willing to see the task through to completion no matter what the cost?
- How would you like God to use you? What would you like a biographer to say about you?
- What would you like your lasting impact on others to be?

a prayer for blessing

Dear Lord,

As I seek to cleanse my hands, O God, purify my heart and make me acceptable in your sight.

I pray that You would look upon me and bless me. As I humble myself before You, exalt me and let Your favor go before me. Spread Your goodness before me. May it accompany Your mercy as it follows me in accordance with Your promises. Lord, cause Your face to shine upon me. Let Your blessings overtake me.

Grant me peace with all who would set their face against me as I walk in peace and fellowship with You. Let no weapon formed against me succeed.

Equip me with the strength to do your will.

Bless the work of my hands and cause me to prosper in all my ways, even as my soul prospers. Order my steps on paths of promotion as I acknowledge You. Grant me the power to gain wealth as I surrender my all to You.

Most of all, I pray that You grant me wisdom. The wisdom to seek You above all things. Teach me to be a wise steward of all You grant, and let each blessing that You render be an occasion to further glorify Your name in the earth.

In the matchless and wonderful name of Jesus.
Amen.

If you would like to correspond with Michelle
in response to her books, contact her at:

Michelle McKinney Hammond
c/o HeartWing Ministries
P.O. Box 11052
Chicago, IL 60611-1722
E-mail: heartwingmin@yahoo.com
Web site: http://www.mckinneyhammond.com or
http://www.heartwing.com

For speaking engagements, contact:
Speak Up Speaker Services
1-888-870-7719